JUMBLE® UNLEASHED

Classic Puzzles

T0096070

JUMBLE®

Unscramble these four Jumbles, one letter to each square, to form four ordinary words.

NAWGO

SPEHE

WYLLOH

TRUSEY

Still wet behind the ears

SUCH RECRUITS HAVE NO BUSINESS GETTING FRESH.

Now arrange the circled letters to form the surprise answer, as suggested by the above cartoon.

Print answer here "◯◯◯" ◯◯◯◯

JUMBLE®

Unscramble these four Jumbles, one letter to each square, to form four ordinary words.

NUWDE

FILOO

RABLER

LURSEY

GRAND OPENING

Now we're in business!

BAR

IT WAS AWFUL—
UNTIL A LETTER
ARRIVED TO MAKE
IT "LEGAL"!

Now arrange the circled letters to form the surprise answer, as suggested by the above cartoon.

Print answer here " ☐ - ☐☐☐☐☐ "

JUMBLE®

Unscramble these four Jumbles, one letter to each square, to form four ordinary words.

WHASA

LULET

INCLEP

TAUBEY

After that (careful!) you'll (watch it!) go and . . .

WHERE HIS WIFE SENT HIM.

Now arrange the circled letters to form the surprise answer, as suggested by the above cartoon.

Print answer here " ◯◯ ◯◯◯ ◯◯◯◯ "

JUMBLE®

Unscramble these four Jumbles, one letter
to each square, to form four ordinary words.

EAPEY

GLOIN

LEHTAH

TREEMP

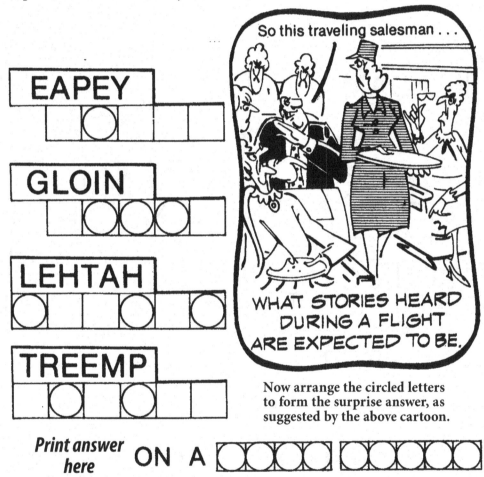

So this traveling salesman . . .

WHAT STORIES HEARD
DURING A FLIGHT
ARE EXPECTED TO BE.

Now arrange the circled letters
to form the surprise answer, as
suggested by the above cartoon.

Print answer here ON A ☐☐☐☐ ☐☐☐☐☐

JUMBLE®

Unscramble these four Jumbles, one letter
to each square, to form four ordinary words.

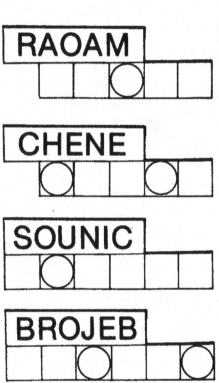

RAOAM

CHENE

SOUNIC

BROJEB

JEWELRY

SHE WANTED THE PIN,
BUT HESITATED
TO DO THIS.

Now arrange the circled letters
to form the surprise answer, as
suggested by the above cartoon.

Print answer here "◯◯◯◯◯◯◯" IT

JUMBLE®

Unscramble these four Jumbles, one letter
to each square, to form four ordinary words.

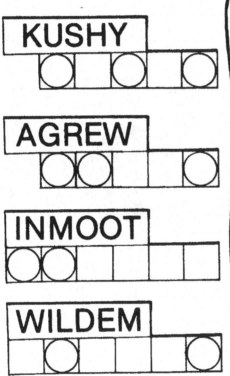

KUSHY

AGREW

INMOOT

WILDEM

He'll probably get
a raise!

A PRETTY LOW FORM
OF LIFE MIGHT GET
AHEAD WHEN HE
DOES THIS.

Now arrange the circled letters
to form the surprise answer, as
suggested by the above cartoon.

Print answer here

JUMBLE®

Unscramble these four Jumbles, one letter
to each square, to form four ordinary words.

KADEB

PADAT

WEDDEG

HASRIG

WHAT "CHANGED" WHEN
THE SNOW MELTED?

Now arrange the circled letters
to form the surprise answer, as
suggested by the above cartoon.

Print answer here " ⬡⬡⬡⬡ "

JUMBLE

Unscramble these four Jumbles, one letter to each square, to form four ordinary words.

ARATO

PEBID

TINBAD

NAMORT

IT MAY BE THE CAUSE OF A KID'S RUNNING AWAY FROM HOME.

Now arrange the circled letters to form the surprise answer, as suggested by the above cartoon.

Print answer here   AN

JUMBLE®

Unscramble these four Jumbles, one letter to each square, to form four ordinary words.

LAMEY

BICUT

ENBRAY

DESMOT

Too big a night?

OUT OF JAIL—AND ILL IN BED.

Now arrange the circled letters to form the surprise answer, as suggested by the above cartoon.

Print answer here "◻-◻◻◻-◻◻"

JUMBLE®

Unscramble these four Jumbles, one letter
to each square, to form four ordinary words.

NILER

SUMIN

GARCHE

NAPMEN

METAL DEVICES
THAT HELP KEEP
LOCKS IN PLACE.

Now arrange the circled letters
to form the surprise answer, as
suggested by the above cartoon.

Print answer here ◯◯◯◯◯◯◯◯◯

JUMBLE®

Unscramble these four Jumbles, one letter
to each square, to form four ordinary words.

SUMEA

ILETT

NILJEG

GAYMIB

WHAT A GIRL
SOMETIMES WEARS
AT THE BEACH.

Now arrange the circled letters
to form the surprise answer, as
suggested by the above cartoon.

Print answer here A

JUMBLE®

Unscramble these four Jumbles, one letter to each square, to form four ordinary words.

LENEK

GALUH

BIMBIE

KOJECY

THEY CALLED HIM A COLORFUL FIGHTER BECAUSE HE WAS THIS MOST OF THE TIME.

Now arrange the circled letters to form the surprise answer, as suggested by the above cartoon.

Print answer here ⬚⬚⬚⬚⬚⬚ & ⬚⬚⬚⬚⬚

JUMBLE

Unscramble these four Jumbles, one letter to each square, to form four ordinary words.

UPTIL

LAHCK

EXGONY

REQUIV

HOW TO DRESS ON A VERY COLD DAY.

Now arrange the circled letters to form the surprise answer, as suggested by the above cartoon.

Print answer here

JUMBLE®

Unscramble these four Jumbles, one letter
to each square, to form four ordinary words.

SETAC

ENMOY

WHYNOA

DILBOE

WHY THE COPS
COULDN'T CATCH
UP WITH THE
PICKPOCKET.

Now arrange the circled letters
to form the surprise answer, as
suggested by the above cartoon.

*Print answer
here*   HE

JUMBLE®

Unscramble these four Jumbles, one letter
to each square, to form four ordinary words.

NOMEW

CUJIE

SWAALY

BRICKE

Ugh!

WHAT THOSE
HOBOES WERE
TELLING.

Now arrange the circled letters
to form the surprise answer, as
suggested by the above cartoon.

Print answer here " ⬡⬡⬡ " ⬡⬡⬡⬡⬡

JUMBLE

Unscramble these four Jumbles, one letter
to each square, to form four ordinary words.

REQUE

GRABE

JURNIY

DORCEF

KOFF   KOFF

WHAT THE HEAVY
SMOKER WAS
ADVISED TO DO.

Now arrange the circled letters
to form the surprise answer, as
suggested by the above cartoon.

Print answer here

JUMBLE ®

Unscramble these four Jumbles, one letter to each square, to form four ordinary words.

SOUHE

ENATE

SHRAIG

GINCHA

WHAT ONE MOUSE SAID TO THE OTHER AS HE SAW THE TRAP BEING BAITED.

Now arrange the circled letters to form the surprise answer, as suggested by the above cartoon.

Print answer here " ◯◯◯◯◯◯ ◯◯ "

JUMBLE®

Unscramble these four Jumbles, one letter to each square, to form four ordinary words.

VINEA

MAROA

RAPTYN

CRALIG

DRY CLEANER

AN ARTICLE OF CLOTHING A GENTLE-MAN MIGHT HAVE AROUND THE ARM.

Now arrange the circled letters to form the surprise answer, as suggested by the above cartoon.

Print answer here " ☐ - ☐☐☐ - ☐☐☐ "

JUMBLE®

Unscramble these four Jumbles, one letter to each square, to form four ordinary words.

FRATE

EKRIP

JYLFOU

LAMTEL

WHAT THE GAMBLER NAMED HIS DAUGHTER.

Now arrange the circled letters to form the surprise answer, as suggested by the above cartoon.

Print answer here

JUMBLE®

Unscramble these four Jumbles, one letter
to each square, to form four ordinary words.

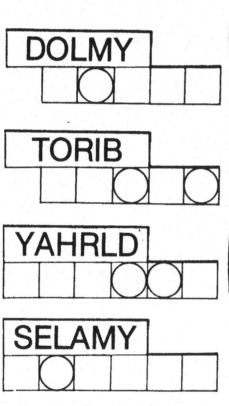

DOLMY

TORIB

YAHRLD

SELAMY

RAN OFF WITH
A ROLL OF
CLOTH.

Now arrange the circled letters
to form the surprise answer, as
suggested by the above cartoon.

Print answer here " ◯◯◯◯◯ – ◯◯ "

JUMBLE®

Unscramble these four Jumbles, one letter to each square, to form four ordinary words.

MUPIO

LOCON

ENGLOB

RETOIG

WHAT'S THE ROYAL ROAD TO MARRIAGE?

Now arrange the circled letters to form the surprise answer, as suggested by the above cartoon.

Print answer here

☐☐☐☐☐ TO " ☐☐☐☐☐ "

JUMBLE®

Unscramble these four Jumbles, one letter to each square, to form four ordinary words.

TARFD

CAMPH

SPICHY

TENCIE

You're wonderful!

Yes, I know

WHAT THAT "SWELL" GUY HAD.

Now arrange the circled letters to form the surprise answer, as suggested by the above cartoon.

Print answer here A ⭕⭕⭕⭕⭕ TO ⭕⭕⭕⭕⭕⭕

JUMBLE®

Unscramble these four Jumbles, one letter
to each square, to form four ordinary words.

CHEEN

SMIPK

MEEDAF

HEETES

WHAT A
MERMAID IS.

Now arrange the circled letters
to form the surprise answer, as
suggested by the above cartoon.

**Print
answer
here** A ⬡⬡⬡⬡⬡ ⬡⬡⬡ – ⬡⬡⬡⬡

JUMBLE®

Unscramble these four Jumbles, one letter
to each square, to form four ordinary words.

NYWEL

GLARN

MILTEY

BUSTIM

Nothing for me

YOU MIGHT SERVE
IT TO OTHERS, BUT
YOU WOULDN'T WANT TO
EAT IT YOURSELF.

Now arrange the circled letters
to form the surprise answer, as
suggested by the above cartoon.

*Print
answer
here*   **A**

JUMBLE®

Unscramble these four Jumbles, one letter
to each square, to form four ordinary words.

VELOR

DIOTT

SEVURS

HARMIO

HONK

HONK

HONK

SPUTTER

WHAT A SOUPED-UP
CAR THAT BROKE
DOWN WAS.

Now arrange the circled letters
to form the surprise answer, as
suggested by the above cartoon.

Print answer here A " ◯◯◯◯◯ " ◯◯◯

JUMBLE®
UNLEASHED

Daily Puzzles

JUMBLE

Unscramble these four Jumbles, one letter
to each square, to form four ordinary words.

IRROG

GUBOH

KEENAW

DYLOOB

SILENCE

WHY THE BOOKWORM
VISITED THE
LIBRARY.

Now arrange the circled letters
to form the surprise answer, as
suggested by the above cartoon.

*Print
answer
here*

TO " _____ " A _____

JUMBLE®

Unscramble these four Jumbles, one letter
to each square, to form four ordinary words.

SIFOT

TYLFO

LIFEED

PETICK

WHAT TWO WORDS
HAVE THE MOST
LETTERS IN THEM?

Now arrange the circled letters
to form the surprise answer, as
suggested by the above cartoon.

Print answer here

JUMBLE®

Unscramble these four Jumbles, one letter
to each square, to form four ordinary words.

DUELE

STUJO

BREEMM

REJUIN

WHAT YOU MIGHT
SEE WHEN A BIG
ELEPHANT SQUIRTS
WATER FROM HIS
TRUNK.

Now arrange the circled letters
to form the surprise answer, as
suggested by the above cartoon.

Print answer here A ☐☐☐☐☐☐ ☐☐☐

JUMBLE®

Unscramble these four Jumbles, one letter to each square, to form four ordinary words.

KAYLE

MOECT

SMEECH

SPOOPE

WHAT **SLOT MACHINES** PRODUCE FOR THEIR OWNERS.

Now arrange the circled letters to form the surprise answer, as suggested by the above cartoon.

Print answer here " ⬡⬡⬡⬡ ⬡⬡⬡⬡ IN ' ⬡⬡ ' "

JUMBLE®

Unscramble these four Jumbles, one letter
to each square, to form four ordinary words.

LAGEE

FOIMT

REBAWE

DENGER

WHAT THE CATTLE
RAISER DID WHEN
HE GOT A
BUM STEER.

Now arrange the circled letters
to form the surprise answer, as
suggested by the above cartoon.

Print answer here ◯◯◯◯◯◯ ABOUT ◯◯

JUMBLE®

Unscramble these four Jumbles, one letter to each square, to form four ordinary words.

SUIGE

TIDEF

YAMBIG

ROCFAT

WHAT HE SAID WHEN HE HEARD HIS NEIGHBOR HAD BOUGHT ONE OF THOSE NEW COMPUTERS.

Now arrange the circled letters to form the surprise answer, as suggested by the above cartoon.

Print answer here ◯◯ ◯◯◯◯◯◯◯ !

JUMBLE®

Unscramble these four Jumbles, one letter
to each square, to form four ordinary words.

UPMEL

POAKK

MIEPED

LOOSCH

WHAT THE TIMID SOUL
FINALLY DID WHEN HIS
BICYCLE WHEEL
COLLAPSED.

Now arrange the circled letters
to form the surprise answer, as
suggested by the above cartoon.

Print answer here "⬭⬭⬭⬭⬭" ⬭⬭

JUMBLE®

Unscramble these four Jumbles, one letter
to each square, to form four ordinary words.

UNYTT

ROALF

SMIDOW

BEATED

WHAT THAT
FILIBUSTERER
IN THE SENATE
WAS THROWING.

Now arrange the circled letters
to form the surprise answer, as
suggested by the above cartoon.

Print
answer
here   HIS "⬡⬡⬡⬡⬡" ⬡⬡⬡⬡⬡⬡⬡

JUMBLE®

Unscramble these four Jumbles, one letter
to each square, to form four ordinary words.

AUZER

COHLT

RUMABI

LICTIE

Beautiful move, dearest

WHAT THE MAN
FROM PRAGUE
CALLED HIS WIFE.

Now arrange the circled letters
to form the surprise answer, as
suggested by the above cartoon.

*Print
answer
here*   HIS " ⬡⬡⬡⬡⬡ " ⬡⬡⬡⬡

JUMBLE®

Unscramble these four Jumbles, one letter to each square, to form four ordinary words.

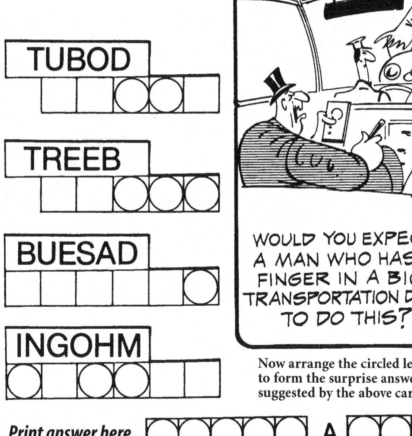

TUBOD

TREEB

BUESAD

INGOHM

WOULD YOU EXPECT A MAN WHO HAS A FINGER IN A BIG TRANSPORTATION DEAL TO DO THIS?

Now arrange the circled letters to form the surprise answer, as suggested by the above cartoon.

Print answer here ⬡⬡⬡⬡⬡ A ⬡⬡⬡⬡

JUMBLE®

Unscramble these four Jumbles, one letter
to each square, to form four ordinary words.

EGGAU

YIRDT

RETHEN

DROINO

WHO WAS THAT
GHOST WHO
APPEARED AT
THE DOOR?

Now arrange the circled letters
to form the surprise answer, as
suggested by the above cartoon.

Print answer here A

JUMBLE®

Unscramble these four Jumbles, one letter
to each square, to form four ordinary words.

DEGEH

TIXYS

GIZZAG

SNEEWT

We'll take it!

FOR A SWEATER, HE
THOUGHT THIS WAS
THE RIGHT SIZE.

Now arrange the circled letters
to form the surprise answer, as
suggested by the above cartoon.

Print answer here THE ☐☐☐☐☐☐ ☐☐☐☐

JUMBLE®

Unscramble these four Jumbles, one letter
to each square, to form four ordinary words.

STEUG

RAAMO

GLUDEE

NERUNG

WHAT SOME BACKSEAT
DRIVERS NEVER
SEEM TO DO.

Now arrange the circled letters
to form the surprise answer, as
suggested by the above cartoon.

**Print answer
here** ☐☐☐ ☐☐☐ OF ☐☐☐

JUMBLE®

Unscramble these four Jumbles, one letter
to each square, to form four ordinary words.

ANCKK

ITTYD

PROOCE

FITHES

HOW TO BRIGHTEN UP
YOUR BOYFRIEND'S
EVENING.

Now arrange the circled letters
to form the surprise answer, as
suggested by the above cartoon.

**Print answer
here** ⬡⬡⬡ ⬡⬡ THE ⬡⬡⬡⬡

JUMBLE®

Unscramble these four Jumbles, one letter
to each square, to form four ordinary words.

GALEL

HOTBO

FRAIDT

WARROM

WHAT THE BLIND DATE
SHE WAS LOOKING
FORWARD TO MEETING
TURNED OUT TO BE.

Now arrange the circled letters
to form the surprise answer, as
suggested by the above cartoon.

*Print
answer
here*   A " ⬡⬡⬡⬡⬡   ⬡⬡⬡⬡⬡ "

JUMBLE

Unscramble these four Jumbles, one letter to each square, to form four ordinary words.

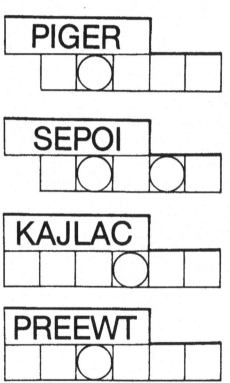

PIGER

SEPOI

KAJLAC

PREEWT

WHAT THE JUDGE GAVE THE GUY WHO WAS ARRESTED FOR STEALING A WATCH.

Now arrange the circled letters to form the surprise answer, as suggested by the above cartoon.

Print answer here THE "  "

JUMBLE®

Unscramble these four Jumbles, one letter to each square, to form four ordinary words.

YEHRM

DAUTI

PHARME

RYNFEZ

CLANG
CLANG

IF SHE EVER TOLD HER REAL AGE, HER BIRTHDAY CAKE WOULD BE THIS.

Now arrange the circled letters to form the surprise answer, as suggested by the above cartoon.

Print answer here A ◯◯◯◯◯ ◯◯◯◯◯◯◯

JUMBLE®

Unscramble these four Jumbles, one letter
to each square, to form four ordinary words.

NARPO

HAWRT

TELSED

PRULAB

IN ORDER TO FIND OUT
WHICH KIND OF ICE-
CREAM SODA IS THE
BEST, TAKE THIS.

Now arrange the circled letters
to form the surprise answer, as
suggested by the above cartoon.

*Print answer
here*   A " ◯◯◯◯◯ " ◯◯◯◯

Unscramble these four Jumbles, one letter to each square, to form four ordinary words.

ROFUL

NAIGG

TACTIN

GERELD

HER FACE IS HER FORTUNE, AND IT RUNS INTO THIS.

Now arrange the circled letters to form the surprise answer, as suggested by the above cartoon.

Print answer here A

JUMBLE®

Unscramble these four Jumbles, one letter to each square, to form four ordinary words.

GHUDO

VELGO

BLOMIE

MECION

Hi, sweetie

NEEDED TO IMPRESS A LAUNDRESS.

Now arrange the circled letters to form the surprise answer, as suggested by the above cartoon.

Print answer here A ◯◯◯◯◯ ◯◯◯◯

JUMBLE®

Unscramble these four Jumbles, one letter to each square, to form four ordinary words.

AVERB

NEYOH

NOAWHY

DEGULC

HE HAD A "PEACH" OF A SECRETARY UNTIL HIS WIFE ORDERED THIS.

Now arrange the circled letters to form the surprise answer, as suggested by the above cartoon.

Print answer here ◯◯◯ " ◯◯◯◯◯◯ "

JUMBLE®

Unscramble these four Jumbles, one letter to each square, to form four ordinary words.

MIRPE

ZYIZD

BREPUS

PREJUM

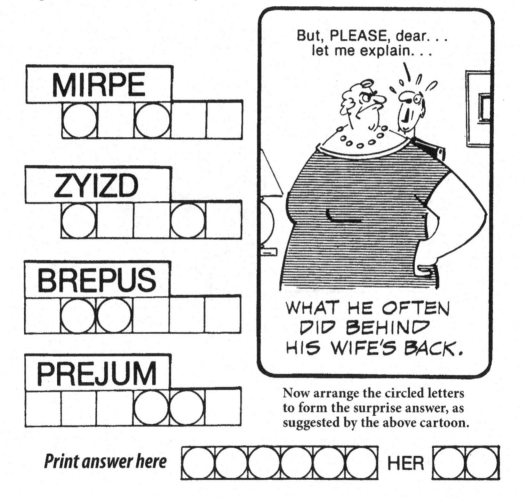

But, PLEASE, dear. . . let me explain. . .

WHAT HE OFTEN DID BEHIND HIS WIFE'S BACK.

Now arrange the circled letters to form the surprise answer, as suggested by the above cartoon.

Print answer here ⬭⬭⬭⬭⬭⬭⬭ HER ⬭⬭

JUMBLE®

Unscramble these four Jumbles, one letter
to each square, to form four ordinary words.

CIHRB

LUCOT

NOYFLE

INDIGH

I demand that my client
continue to be supported
in the manner to which she
has been accustomed

WHY HIS EX-WIFE
TOOK HIM TO
THE CLEANERS.

Now arrange the circled letters
to form the surprise answer, as
suggested by the above cartoon.

*Print
answer
here*   HE WAS ◯◯◯◯◯◯◯ ◯◯◯◯◯

JUMBLE®

Unscramble these four Jumbles, one letter to each square, to form four ordinary words.

ORRGI

GUNDE

NELPOY

FLUTAR

THEY RESENTED THAT RITZY POOCH BECAUSE HE ALWAYS WANTED TO DO THIS.

Now arrange the circled letters to form the surprise answer, as suggested by the above cartoon.

Print answer here ⬡⬡⬡ ON THE ⬡⬡⬡

JUMBLE

Unscramble these four Jumbles, one letter
to each square, to form four ordinary words.

INCCY

VENAH

SPOCER

EMBURP

WAYS THAT GO
STRAIGHT TO
THE HEART.

Now arrange the circled letters
to form the surprise answer, as
suggested by the above cartoon.

Print answer here ◯◯◯◯◯

JUMBLE®

Unscramble these four Jumbles, one letter
to each square, to form four ordinary words.

TIDIO

HECEK

PRETOY

DILVER

But I didn't do nothin'!

HOW HE PROTESTED
WHEN THEY PUT
HIM IN THE COOLER.

Now arrange the circled letters
to form the surprise answer, as
suggested by the above cartoon.

Print answer here

JUMBLE®

Unscramble these four Jumbles, one letter
to each square, to form four ordinary words.

DORBO

MYLOD

PLECOM

CIVONE

—How dare you!—

THE SNOB WAS
INSULTED WHEN THE
DOCTOR TOLD HIM
HE WAS MERELY SUF-
FERING FROM THIS.

Now arrange the circled letters
to form the surprise answer, as
suggested by the above cartoon.

Print an-
swer here A " ◯◯◯◯◯◯ " ◯◯◯◯

JUMBLE®

Unscramble these four Jumbles, one letter
to each square, to form four ordinary words.

LAMDY

KERPI

EPSOOP

BEPSIC

It's him again! Won't be in.
CLAIMS he's not feeling well

IT MIGHT BE
"ILL-GOTTEN."

Now arrange the circled letters
to form the surprise answer, as
suggested by the above cartoon.

Print answer here

JUMBLE®

Unscramble these four Jumbles, one letter
to each square, to form four ordinary words.

UNOMT

JETEC

TASTLE

HATTOR

HOSPITAL

MIGHT BE THREE
THAT COULD PUT
YOU OUT.

Now arrange the circled letters
to form the surprise answer, as
suggested by the above cartoon.

Print answer here " "

JUMBLE®

Unscramble these four Jumbles, one letter
to each square, to form four ordinary words.

TRIVE

PRIVE

NIVIET

HUNCAL

We always assure a good reception here

THE WARDEN GUAR-
ANTEED THE ENTER-
TAINERS THAT THE
AUDIENCE WOULD
BE THIS.

Now arrange the circled letters
to form the surprise answer, as
suggested by the above cartoon.

Print answer here A " ⬡⬡⬡⬡⬡⬡⬡ " ONE

JUMBLE®

Unscramble these four Jumbles, one letter
to each square, to form four ordinary words.

CELEX

NAPCI

PHEWEN

KANTLE

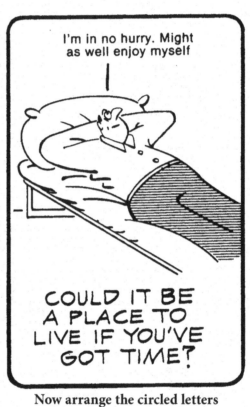

I'm in no hurry. Might
as well enjoy myself

COULD IT BE
A PLACE TO
LIVE IF YOU'VE
GOT TIME?

Now arrange the circled letters
to form the surprise answer, as
suggested by the above cartoon.

Print answer here

JUMBLE®

Unscramble these four Jumbles, one letter to each square, to form four ordinary words.

CANKS

RIPPE

COSTAM

LINCEY

THEY HUSH UP REPORTS OF MURDERS.

Now arrange the circled letters to form the surprise answer, as suggested by the above cartoon.

Print answer here

JUMBLE®

Unscramble these four Jumbles, one letter
to each square, to form four ordinary words.

CHATY

ROPEA

WAIRND

SILAAS

THIS MUSICAL COM-
POSITION "INVOLVES"
HARPS AT FIRST.

Now arrange the circled letters
to form the surprise answer, as
suggested by the above cartoon.

Print answer " ⬜⬜⬜⬜⬜ – ⬜⬜⬜ "
here

JUMBLE®

Unscramble these four Jumbles, one letter
to each square, to form four ordinary words.

GORAC

SCUFO

THOUPS

OTHPRY

WHAT THE ROOKIE G.I.
WAS TOLD TO TAKE IN
ORDER TO GET TO
THE BARBER'S IN THE
QUICKEST POSSIBLE WAY.

Now arrange the circled letters
to form the surprise answer, as
suggested by the above cartoon.

Print answer here A ◯◯◯◯◯◯ ◯◯◯

JUMBLE®

Unscramble these four Jumbles, one letter
to each square, to form four ordinary words.

RANOB

FLOTY

BITSUM

LISGRY

WHAT "JACK AND THE
BEANSTALK" IS.

Now arrange the circled letters
to form the surprise answer, as
suggested by the above cartoon.

**Print answer
here**   A

JUMBLE®

Unscramble these four Jumbles, one letter
to each square, to form four ordinary words.

BAXOR

YORFT

PLESIV

QUOPEA

COULD BE A SPORT
"CONNECTED" WITH
THE CLERGY.

Now arrange the circled letters
to form the surprise answer, as
suggested by the above cartoon.

Print answer here "  "

JUMBLE®

Unscramble these four Jumbles, one letter
to each square, to form four ordinary words.

YASTT

DROAR

REYYAL

HOGBUT

But where's my check?

WHAT THEY PAID
THE KING WHO
WROTE A BOOK.

Now arrange the circled letters
to form the surprise answer, as
suggested by the above cartoon.

Print answer here A ⬡⬡⬡⬡⬡⬡⬡

JUMBLE®

Unscramble these four Jumbles, one letter
to each square, to form four ordinary words.

PERIT

ELVOH

GOSTEO

FOUTTI

WHAT THE GUY WHO
STOLE A BANANA
GAVE THE COPS.

Now arrange the circled letters
to form the surprise answer, as
suggested by the above cartoon.

Print answer here

JUMBLE®

Unscramble these four Jumbles, one letter to each square, to form four ordinary words.

KREAM

VALAN

PLATEA

DRAUWP

COULD IT HAVE BEEN A DRAMA ABOUT A FAMOUS FLEET?

Now arrange the circled letters to form the surprise answer, as suggested by the above cartoon.

Print answer here " ◯◯◯◯◯◯ "

JUMBLE®

Unscramble these four Jumbles, one letter
to each square, to form four ordinary words.

GINOR

BREHT

DOHOKE

SENTOL

WHAT HE WAS,
AFTER HE BOUGHT
HER THAT BIG
DIAMOND.

Now arrange the circled letters
to form the surprise answer, as
suggested by the above cartoon.

*Print answer
here* ⬡⬡⬡⬡⬡ – ⬡⬡⬡⬡⬡

JUMBLE®

Unscramble these four Jumbles, one letter
to each square, to form four ordinary words.

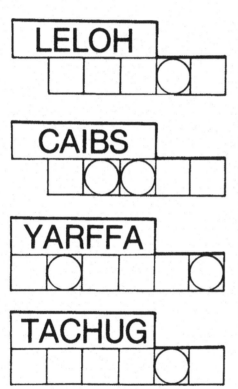

LELOH

CAIBS

YARFFA

TACHUG

Ain't he something?

WHAT KIND OF A GUY WAS THAT PRESS PHOTOGRAPHER?

Now arrange the circled letters
to form the surprise answer, as
suggested by the above cartoon.

Print answer here A  ONE

JUMBLE®

Unscramble these four Jumbles, one letter to each square, to form four ordinary words.

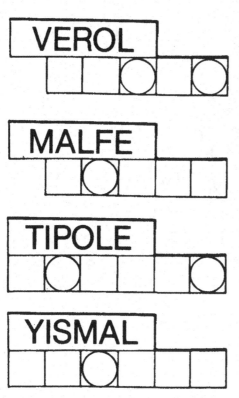

VEROL

MALFE

TIPOLE

YISMAL

Next!

COUNSELOR

HE WORKS OUT
THE PROBLEMS OF
"MIXED-UP" LOVERS.

Now arrange the circled letters to form the surprise answer, as suggested by the above cartoon.

Print answer here

JUMBLE®

Unscramble these four Jumbles, one letter
to each square, to form four ordinary words.

NOICT

POSOT

INSOOP

SOUNIC

EVERYTHING YOU
SHOULD KNOW ABOUT
ENTRANCES AND
EXITS.

Now arrange the circled letters
to form the surprise answer, as
suggested by the above cartoon.

Print answer here   THE ◯◯◯ & ◯◯◯◯◯

JUMBLE®

Unscramble these four Jumbles, one letter to each square, to form four ordinary words.

NIGGO

MONDE

CHYPIS

AFDACE

WHAT THAT MUTT LIKED BEST FOR BREAKFAST.

Now arrange the circled letters to form the surprise answer, as suggested by the above cartoon.

Print an-swer here " ◯◯◯◯◯◯◯ " ◯◯◯◯

JUMBLE®

Unscramble these four Jumbles, one letter
to each square, to form four ordinary words.

VARFO

TYIED

INTOOM

PAICEE

WHAT THE GREEK GOD
DID WHEN ONE OF THE
GODDESSES BROUGHT
HIM HIS DRINK.

Now arrange the circled letters
to form the surprise answer, as
suggested by the above cartoon.

Print answer here " ◯◯◯◯◯◯ "

JUMBLE®

Unscramble these four Jumbles, one letter
to each square, to form four ordinary words.

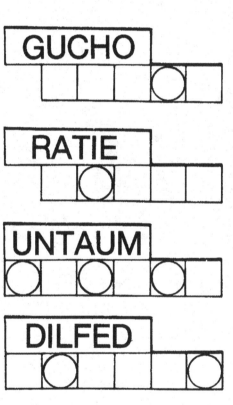

GUCHO

RATIE

UNTAUM

DILFED

CONCERT TON

WHAT TIME IS IT
WHEN CLOTHES
WEAR OUT?

Now arrange the circled letters
to form the surprise answer, as
suggested by the above cartoon.

Print answer here

JUMBLE®

Unscramble these four Jumbles, one letter to each square, to form four ordinary words.

NOUCE

YADIL

HUTORF

YARPTS

WHAT THEY CALLED THAT INTELLECTUAL HOBO.

Now arrange the circled letters to form the surprise answer, as suggested by the above cartoon.

Print answer here THE "⬡⬡⬡⬡ ⬡⬡⬡⬡⬡⬡⬡"

JUMBLE®

Unscramble these four Jumbles, one letter
to each square, to form four ordinary words.

NEKIF

WIHSS

RAGUTI

DECORF

This is no laughing matter!

WHAT ICE ON
THE ROAD IS.

Now arrange the circled letters
to form the surprise answer, as
suggested by the above cartoon.

Print answer here

JUMBLE

Unscramble these four Jumbles, one letter
to each square, to form four ordinary words.

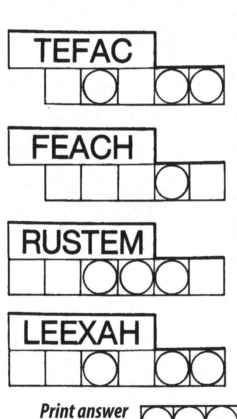

TEFAC

FEACH

RUSTEM

LEEXAH

MANY A "TRUE"
WORD IS SPOKEN
BETWEEN THEM.

Now arrange the circled letters
to form the surprise answer, as
suggested by the above cartoon.

Print answer here

JUMBLE®

Unscramble these four Jumbles, one letter
to each square, to form four ordinary words.

KLACH

METHY

FLOAFY

TANIED

SKIING IS A
WINTERTIME SPORT
OFTEN LEARNED THUS.

Now arrange the circled letters
to form the surprise answer, as
suggested by the above cartoon.

*Print answer
here*   ⬡⬡ ⬡⬡⬡ "⬡⬡⬡⬡"

JUMBLE®

Unscramble these four Jumbles, one letter
to each square, to form four ordinary words.

WADAR

TELOX

KOECIO

EXNOST

WHAT HAPPENED WHEN
THAT BODY BUILDER
PUT A TIGHT T-SHIRT
ON HIS TORSO?

Now arrange the circled letters
to form the surprise answer, as
suggested by the above cartoon.

Print answer here

JUMBLE®

Unscramble these four Jumbles, one letter to each square, to form four ordinary words.

ROWNC

TEBER

SAILEY

ENTHIZ

WHAT THE MAD CHEF WAS.

Now arrange the circled letters to form the surprise answer, as suggested by the above cartoon.

Print answer here

JUMBLE®

Unscramble these four Jumbles, one letter
to each square, to form four ordinary words.

BAYBE

FLABE

LABEZA

TAUBEY

WHAT A FAT
CAT IS.

Now arrange the circled letters
to form the surprise answer, as
suggested by the above cartoon.

*Print an-
swer here* A

JUMBLE®

Unscramble these four Jumbles, one letter to each square, to form four ordinary words.

YUINF

TEAHB

FALLOR

ORCEAN

UNFAIR

WHAT THERE WAS WHEN THE KING OF BEASTS LED A BREAKOUT FROM THE ZOO.

Now arrange the circled letters to form the surprise answer, as suggested by the above cartoon.

Print answer here A " ☐☐☐☐☐☐ - ☐☐☐☐☐ "

JUMBLE®

Unscramble these four Jumbles, one letter
to each square, to form four ordinary words.

SUPIO

RAYPH

INNACE

WORDSY

WHAT TURTLE
SOUP IS.

Now arrange the circled letters
to form the surprise answer, as
suggested by the above cartoon.

*Print answer
here* A

JUMBLE®

Unscramble these four Jumbles, one letter
to each square, to form four ordinary words.

PINTE

DAKEB

NIAMEA

SUTTRY

SALES RESISTANCE
IS THE TRIUMPH
OF THIS.

Now arrange the circled letters
to form the surprise answer, as
suggested by the above cartoon.

*Print an-
swer here* ⬜⭕⭕⭕⭕ OVER ⭕⭕⭕⭕⭕⭕⭕

JUMBLE®

Unscramble these four Jumbles, one letter
to each square, to form four ordinary words.

EFING

HOCAM

HIALAD

SNUIGE

Sorry

WHAT THAT PRETTY
GIRL WHOSE BOY-
FRIEND KEPT HER
WAITING WAS.

Now arrange the circled letters
to form the surprise answer, as
suggested by the above cartoon.

Print an-
swer here A ◯◯◯◯◯◯◯ " ◯◯◯◯ "

JUMBLE®

Unscramble these four Jumbles, one letter
to each square, to form four ordinary words.

BREEL

TRIDY

FISHMA

KLAYEC

HOW SHE LOVED
THE CARDIOLOGIST.

Now arrange the circled letters
to form the surprise answer, as
suggested by the above cartoon.

Print answer here WITH ◯◯◯ HER ◯◯◯◯◯

JUMBLE®

Unscramble these four Jumbles, one letter
to each square, to form four ordinary words.

KEREC

AXMMI

SAYMUL

EXLANF

Stop!

WHAT THE ROBBER
SAID AS HE MADE
HIS GETAWAY.

Now arrange the circled letters
to form the surprise answer, as
suggested by the above cartoon.

**Print answer
here** " ⬡⬡⬡⬡ " BY A ⬡⬡⬡⬡

JUMBLE®

Unscramble these four Jumbles, one letter
to each square, to form four ordinary words.

SOINY

MENGO

YABSUW

TEKLET

EVEN MORE FUN
THAN HAVING A
VACATION IS
HAVING THIS.

Now arrange the circled letters
to form the surprise answer, as
suggested by the above cartoon.

*Print an-
swer here* THE ⬡⬡⬡⬡ ⬡⬡⬡⬡ ⬡⬡⬡

JUMBLE®

Unscramble these four Jumbles, one letter
to each square, to form four ordinary words.

THACC

FETHY

ZELZIF

GLARBE

WHAT THE GUY
WHO THOUGHT HE
WAS A WIT WAS.

Now arrange the circled letters
to form the surprise answer, as
suggested by the above cartoon.

*Print answer
here*   ONLY ☐☐☐☐☐ ☐☐☐☐☐☐

JUMBLE®

Unscramble these four Jumbles, one letter
to each square, to form four ordinary words.

SEHCS

NUWDE

YERSIM

WUNTAL

SHE ADMITTED
SHE WAS FORTY
BUT SHE DIDN'T
DO THIS.

Now arrange the circled letters
to form the surprise answer, as
suggested by the above cartoon.

Print answer here

JUMBLE.

Unscramble these four Jumbles, one letter
to each square, to form four ordinary words.

GOGSY

HAABS

ZELPUZ

GARAVE

WHAT HE SAID
THAT SO-CALLED
BARLEY SOUP WAS.

Now arrange the circled letters
to form the surprise answer, as
suggested by the above cartoon.

**Print answer
here**

JUMBLE®

Unscramble these four Jumbles, one letter
to each square, to form four ordinary words.

WHOSY

MOWNE

ATJECK

SALWAY

WHAT THE TALKING
CAT SAID EVERY
TIME ITS MASTER
RETURNED HOME.

Now arrange the circled letters
to form the surprise answer, as
suggested by the above cartoon.

*Print answer
here* ◯◯◯◯'◯ "◯◯◯"?

JUMBLE®

Unscramble these four Jumbles, one letter
to each square, to form four ordinary words.

KEJOR

YEMON

RAYPER

DEVAUL

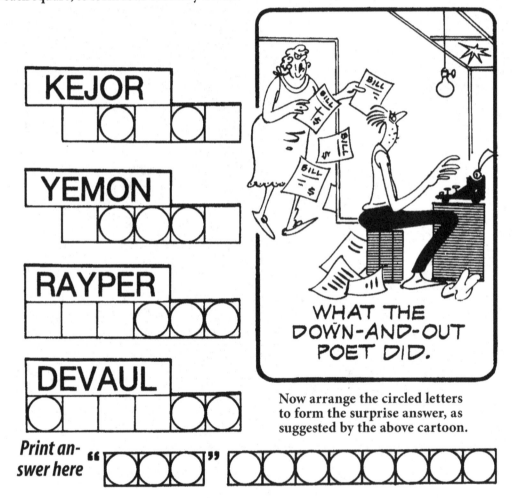

WHAT THE
DOWN-AND-OUT
POET DID.

Now arrange the circled letters
to form the surprise answer, as
suggested by the above cartoon.

*Print an-
swer here* " ☐☐☐ " ☐☐☐☐☐☐☐☐☐

JUMBLE®

Unscramble these four Jumbles, one letter
to each square, to form four ordinary words.

MAWPS

NAJOB

NERRED

EGMAIP

AT WHAT AGE
WERE THEY
MARRIED?

Now arrange the circled letters
to form the surprise answer, as
suggested by the above cartoon.

*Print an-
swer here* AT
THE " ◯◯◯◯◯◯ – ◯◯◯ "

JUMBLE®

Unscramble these four Jumbles, one letter
to each square, to form four ordinary words.

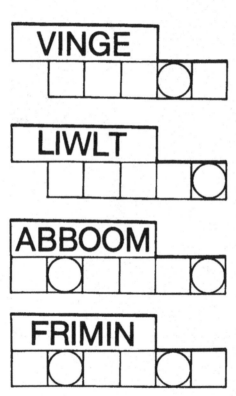

VINGE

LIWLT

ABBOOM

FRIMIN

How about
joining us?

No . . . not
for me

WHAT THE SOLITARY
PAWNBROKER
UNDOUBTEDLY WAS.

Now arrange the circled letters
to form the surprise answer, as
suggested by the above cartoon.

Print answer here A "  "

JUMBLE

Unscramble these four Jumbles, one letter
to each square, to form four ordinary words.

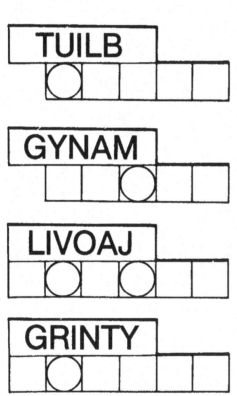

TUILB

GYNAM

LIVOAJ

GRINTY

COULD THIS BE
WHY HE WAS
A JAILBIRD?

Now arrange the circled letters
to form the surprise answer, as
suggested by the above cartoon.

Print answer here

Unscramble these four Jumbles, one letter to each square, to form four ordinary words.

EMICH

UGGEA

CUNBOE

FLOAWL

SOME PEOPLE WHO THINK THEY'RE VERY FUNNY ARE REALLY JUST THIS.

Now arrange the circled letters to form the surprise answer, as suggested by the above cartoon.

Print answer here

JUMBLE®

Unscramble these four Jumbles, one letter to each square, to form four ordinary words.

CYDEA

MABLY

GLUEED

FEXPIR

Er . . . ah . . .

WOMEN A CONFIRMED BACHELOR LEARNS TO AVOID.

Now arrange the circled letters to form the surprise answer, as suggested by the above cartoon.

Print answer here "◯◯◯◯◯◯ – ◯◯◯◯" ONES

JUMBLE®

Unscramble these four Jumbles, one letter
to each square, to form four ordinary words.

GINES

DUGOH

MECENT

SNIULF

You! Out!

THE TROMBONE
PLAYER WAS FIRED
BECAUSE HE
DID THIS.

Now arrange the circled letters
to form the surprise answer, as
suggested by the above cartoon.

*Print an-
swer here* LET

JUMBLE®

Unscramble these four Jumbles, one letter
to each square, to form four ordinary words.

TUNYT

USTEA

LACKAJ

TOORRA

WHAT THEY TOLD
AT THE FOOT
DOCTORS' ANNUAL
SHINDIG.

Now arrange the circled letters
to form the surprise answer, as
suggested by the above cartoon.

*Print an-
swer here* " ⬡⬡⬡⬡⬡ " ⬡⬡⬡⬡⬡

JUMBLE®

Unscramble these four Jumbles, one letter
to each square, to form four ordinary words.

LOJYL

GLIYN

MANALY

SYMFIL

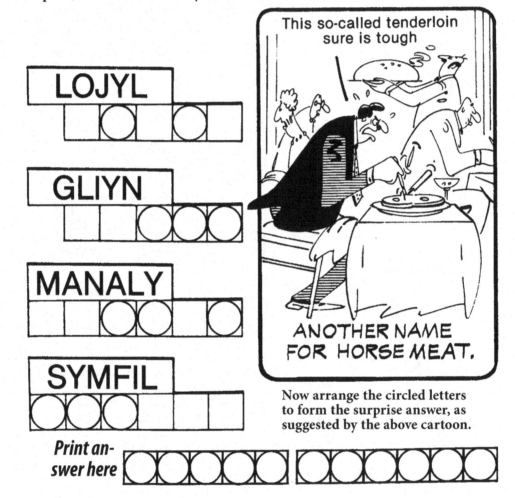

This so-called tenderloin
sure is tough

ANOTHER NAME
FOR HORSE MEAT.

Now arrange the circled letters
to form the surprise answer, as
suggested by the above cartoon.

Print an-
swer here

JUMBLE®

Unscramble these four Jumbles, one letter
to each square, to form four ordinary words.

DOPKE

YANDD

YONDOB

GYABIM

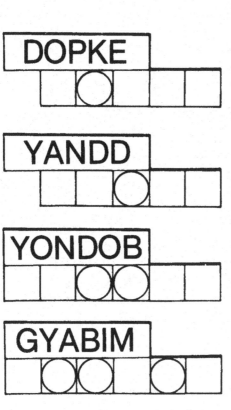

WHAT BUSINESS WAS
AT THE DYNAMITE
FACTORY.

Now arrange the circled letters
to form the surprise answer, as
suggested by the above cartoon.

Print answer here

JUMBLE®

Unscramble these four Jumbles, one letter
to each square, to form four ordinary words.

LAWRB

PUDMY

DAHLER

GLAARN

HONK!

WHAT IT MIGHT
BE WHEN YOU
GAMBOL ACROSS
THE STREET.

Now arrange the circled letters
to form the surprise answer, as
suggested by the above cartoon.

Print answer here

102

JUMBLE®

Unscramble these four Jumbles, one letter
to each square, to form four ordinary words.

SEEAC

DAVPE

REVANT

DERNTY

TANGO TOURNAMENT

Looks like we're all here tonight.

EVERYONE DOING THE
TANGO AT THE CLUB
WAS IN ---

Now arrange the circled letters
to form the surprise answer, as
suggested by the above cartoon.

Print an-
swer here "⬡⬡⬡⬡⬡⬡-⬡⬡⬡⬡⬡"

JUMBLE

Unscramble these four Jumbles, one letter
to each square, to form four ordinary words.

KCALF

TOAIR

SLUHDO

NETOPT

This will be the first
of eighteen lessons.
First, you need to get
a feel for the history.
Swing this.

Can we go to
the practice
range first?

HE WANTED TO LEARN
HOW TO PLAY GOLF,
SO HE ---

Now arrange the circled letters
to form the surprise answer, as
suggested by the above cartoon.

*Print an-
swer here*

JUMBLE®

Unscramble these four Jumbles, one letter
to each square, to form four ordinary words.

LOVEW

CEWIT

CLAKET

AMURDI

The design calls for taller doorways for the giraffes.

Giraffes! What giraffes?

WHEN NOAH DESIGNED HIS HUGE BOAT, HE WAS AN ----

Now arrange the circled letters
to form the surprise answer, as
suggested by the above cartoon.

Print an-
swer here " ◯◯◯ - ◯◯◯◯◯ "

JUMBLE®

Unscramble these four Jumbles, one letter
to each square, to form four ordinary words.

NTIHN

GROOF

VOMREE

TOONIN

So, does this make the final cut?

This one is definitely in the running.

For Sale

THEY HADN'T YET DECIDED
WHICH NEW HOUSE TO BUY,
BUT THEY WERE ----

Now arrange the circled letters
to form the surprise answer, as
suggested by the above cartoon.

Print an-
swer here

JUMBLE®

Unscramble these four Jumbles, one letter
to each square, to form four ordinary words.

GINAA

GORAC

WAMODE

LUDMOE

I need two Caesars.

Relax! It will be all right. We'll run to the market around the corner.

We're out! What do we do?

We're sunk!

WHEN THEY RAN OUT OF
LETTUCE FOR SALADS, HE
TOLD THE KITCHEN STAFF
TO ---

Now arrange the circled letters
to form the surprise answer, as
suggested by the above cartoon.

*Print an-
swer here* " ☐☐☐☐☐☐☐☐ " ☐☐☐☐

JUMBLE®

Unscramble these four Jumbles, one letter
to each square, to form four ordinary words.

TYSUM

MENOV

BORREB

GIROIN

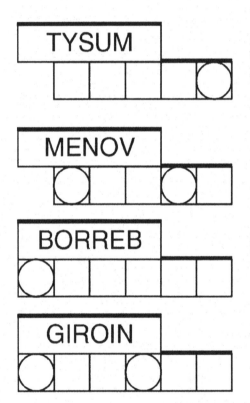

These are so cool!

I can't believe the song fits on one of these.

Be careful not to scratch it.

IN THE 1950'S, 45 RPM RECORDS BECAME SO POPULAR BECAUSE PEOPLE THOUGHT THEY WERE———

Now arrange the circled letters
to form the surprise answer, as
suggested by the above cartoon.

Print answer here

JUMBLE®

Unscramble these four Jumbles, one letter
to each square, to form four ordinary words.

MIREG

DUHON

VITENA

BALIVE

SOUTHEASTERN SWIM SCHOOL

Syd's showing no fear.

That didn't take long.

Here I come!

I've got you.

WHEN IT CAME TO LEARNING
HOW TO SWIM, SHE WAS
READY TO ----

Now arrange the circled letters
to form the surprise answer, as
suggested by the above cartoon.

**Print an-
swer here**

JUMBLE®

Unscramble these four Jumbles, one letter to each square, to form four ordinary words.

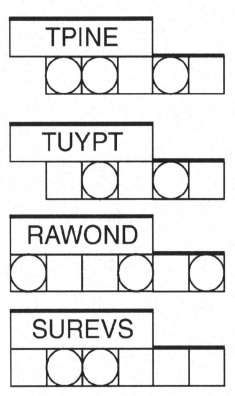

TPINE

TUYPT

RAWOND

SUREVS

Wow! We're at 5,400 feet.

It says that this is the highest point in the state.

THEY WANTED MORE INFORMATION ABOUT THE MOUNTAIN THEY'D JUST CLIMBED, SO THEY ----

Now arrange the circled letters to form the surprise answer, as suggested by the above cartoon.

Print answer here

JUMBLE®

Unscramble these four Jumbles, one letter
to each square, to form four ordinary words.

GEDHE

TOHMU

MEROYM

LEESAW

Hi, honey! I'm so glad
to be here. It was a
great trip.

I'm so glad
you're back!

THE OWNER OF THE
HAWAIIAN SUGAR
PLANTATION WAS ----

Now arrange the circled letters
to form the surprise answer, as
suggested by the above cartoon.

*Print an-
swer here*

111

JUMBLE®

Unscramble these four Jumbles, one letter
to each square, to form four ordinary words.

LAFWU

WENDU

LOOIER

APINDU

It says here that
the Limbo is a
traditional
popular dance
contest that
originated on
the island of
Trinidad.

I had no idea.

Limbo

THE WIKIPEDIA PAGE ABOUT
THE HISTORY OF THE LIMBO
FEATURED THE ---

Now arrange the circled letters
to form the surprise answer, as
suggested by the above cartoon.

Print answer here ◯◯◯ - ◯◯◯◯

JUMBLE®

Unscramble these four Jumbles, one letter to each square, to form four ordinary words.

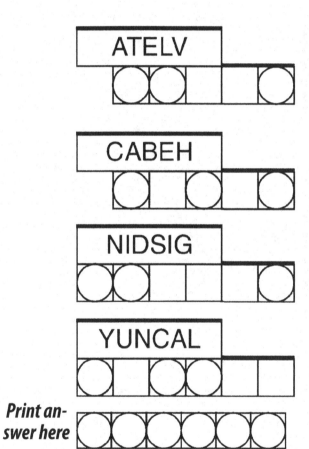

ATELV

CABEH

NIDSIG

YUNCAL

Are you enjoying yourselves?

Yes! Oooh!

EVERYONE WATCHING THE 4TH OF JULY FIREWORKS DISPLAY WAS ---

Now arrange the circled letters to form the surprise answer, as suggested by the above cartoon.

Print answer here

JUMBLE®

Unscramble these four Jumbles, one letter to each square, to form four ordinary words.

GUFED

VORPE

DENGEL

SLUYJT

We have no room. We're never going to be able to sleep like this.

I know. We have to try. It's going to be morning when we arrive.

FLYING ON THE CRAMPED PLANE TO ITALY LEFT THEM ––––

Now arrange the circled letters to form the surprise answer, as suggested by the above cartoon.

Print answer here ◯◯◯ " ◯◯◯◯◯◯ "

JUMBLE®

Unscramble these four Jumbles, one letter to each square, to form four ordinary words.

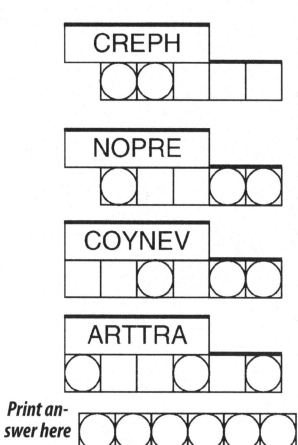

CREPH

NOPRE

COYNEV

ARTTRA

Will it be Euros or credit card?

Sounds great.

Can we get some gelato?

This much for pasta?

THE HIGH PRICE OF THEIR PASTA DINNER IN FLORENCE COST THEM A ----

Now arrange the circled letters to form the surprise answer, as suggested by the above cartoon.

Print answer here

" "

JUMBLE

Unscramble these four Jumbles, one letter to each square, to form four ordinary words.

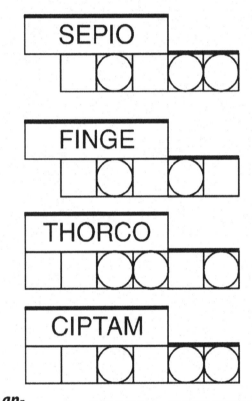

SEPIO

FINGE

THORCO

CIPTAM

Scusarci.

We're looking for some great gelato.

I can tell you about a place that no tourists know about.

THEY ASKED THE REPORTER WHERE TO BUY THE BEST GELATO, SO THEY COULD ----

Now arrange the circled letters to form the surprise answer, as suggested by the above cartoon.

Print answer here

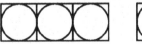  

JUMBLE®

Unscramble these four Jumbles, one letter
to each square, to form four ordinary words.

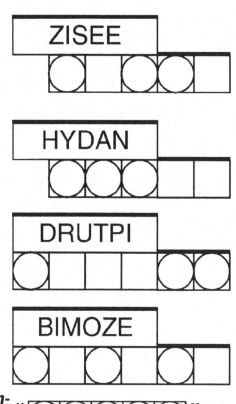

ZISEE

HYDAN

DRUTPI

BIMOZE

That's not a pie! How
can you even call that
a slice?

No one
asked you!
Get out!

WHEN THE CUSTOMER AT
THE ITALIAN EATERY GOT
ANGRY, HE GAVE THE
OWNER A ---

Now arrange the circled letters
to form the surprise answer, as
suggested by the above cartoon.

**Print an-
swer here** "  " OF

JUMBLE®

Unscramble these four Jumbles, one letter
to each square, to form four ordinary words.

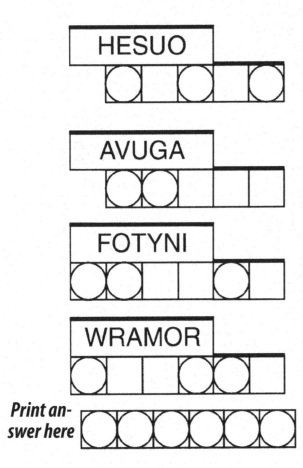

HESUO

AVUGA

FOTYNI

WRAMOR

This is where all of Rome would meet.

Do you kids want to be in the picture?

I'm so tired of ruins!

I'm done!

SEEING ROMAN RUINS ALL DAY WAS THIS FOR THE TEENAGERS.

Now arrange the circled letters
to form the surprise answer, as
suggested by the above cartoon.

Print answer here " "

JUMBLE®

Unscramble these four Jumbles, one letter
to each square, to form four ordinary words.

OAKAL

PITOL

CHURGO

HORLEL

GOING THROUGH THE
GIFT SHOP AT THE MUSEUM
WAS A ---

Now arrange the circled letters
to form the surprise answer, as
suggested by the above cartoon.

Print answer here

JUMBLE®

Unscramble these four Jumbles, one letter to each square, to form four ordinary words.

MUUSH

NICIG

SAROBB

CEFTDE

Well, it took a while to save for these, but this roof will be worth it.

JIM WILSON CONSTRUCTION

TO PAY FOR THE NEW ROOF SUPPORT SYSTEM, HE USED HIS ---

Now arrange the circled letters to form the surprise answer, as suggested by the above cartoon.

Print answer here " ⬡⬡⬡⬡⬡ " ⬡⬡⬡⬡

JUMBLE®

Unscramble these four Jumbles, one letter
to each square, to form four ordinary words.

LUDAT

SCURH

LEYREF

BERHEY

I'm going around to
the other side of the
pasture today.

AFTER SEEING HOW ANGRY
THE MALE COW WAS, SHE
DECIDED TO ---

Now arrange the circled letters
to form the surprise answer, as
suggested by the above cartoon.

*Print an-
swer here*

JUMBLE®

Unscramble these four Jumbles, one letter to each square, to form four ordinary words.

SADAL

GIRNB

GLUPEN

RREFOV

At 78 years old, it's built to last.

7/15

HUNDREDS OF MILLIONS OF CARS HAVE CROSSED THE GOLDEN GATE BRIDGE, THANKS TO ITS ----

Now arrange the circled letters to form the surprise answer, as suggested by the above cartoon.

Print answer here

JUMBLE®

Unscramble these four Jumbles, one letter to each square, to form four ordinary words.

GUNOY

CUVHO

NEVNEU

DRAYHL

They need to get a tree.

I think it's sweet.

THE AFFECTIONATE PIGEONS WERE ----

Now arrange the circled letters to form the surprise answer, as suggested by the above cartoon.

Print answer here

⬡⬡⬡⬡⬡ - ⬡⬡⬡⬡⬡⬡

JUMBLE®

Unscramble these four Jumbles, one letter to each square, to form four ordinary words.

WENHI

ASAIL

FARDIA

FYMSIL

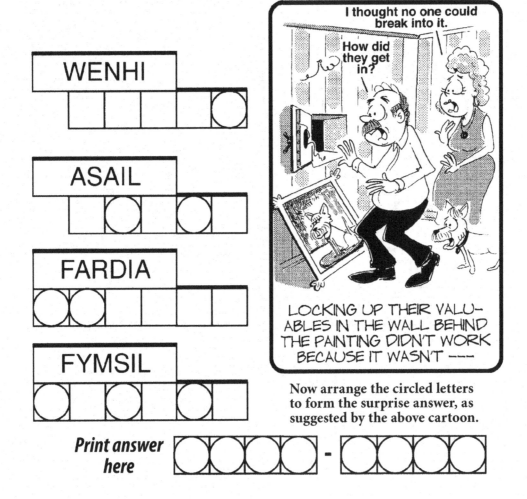

I thought no one could break into it.

How did they get in?

LOCKING UP THEIR VALU-ABLES IN THE WALL BEHIND THE PAINTING DIDN'T WORK BECAUSE IT WASN'T ---

Now arrange the circled letters to form the surprise answer, as suggested by the above cartoon.

Print answer here ◯◯◯◯◯ - ◯◯◯◯

JUMBLE®

Unscramble these four Jumbles, one letter to each square, to form four ordinary words.

NODWU

SNUTT

DOANIJ

DROYAP

THE OWNERS OF THE NEW PLANT NURSERY HAD NO PLANS TO EVER MOVE AND WANTED TO ---

Now arrange the circled letters to form the surprise answer, as suggested by the above cartoon.

Print answer here

JUMBLE®

Unscramble these four Jumbles, one letter
to each square, to form four ordinary words.

MOCEA

TUCEA

SKROEH

TREIMH

You both have similar skills. I think you'd enjoy playing each other.

How about it?

Ace told me you have a great serve.

WHEN HE PAIRED THE
TWO PLAYERS, THE
TENNIS PRO WAS A ---

Now arrange the circled letters
to form the surprise answer, as
suggested by the above cartoon.

*Print an-
swer here*

JUMBLE®

Unscramble these four Jumbles, one letter
to each square, to form four ordinary words.

VARWE

RRULA

PREPAA

VIOTEM

your MOVE oVING C

We're booked solid. We need another truck.

Things are really moving.

HIS MOVING BUSINESS REALLY STARTED TO TAKE OFF WHEN THE NUMBER OF JOBS STARTED TO ---

Now arrange the circled letters
to form the surprise answer, as
suggested by the above cartoon.

Print answer here

JUMBLE®

Unscramble these four Jumbles, one letter to each square, to form four ordinary words.

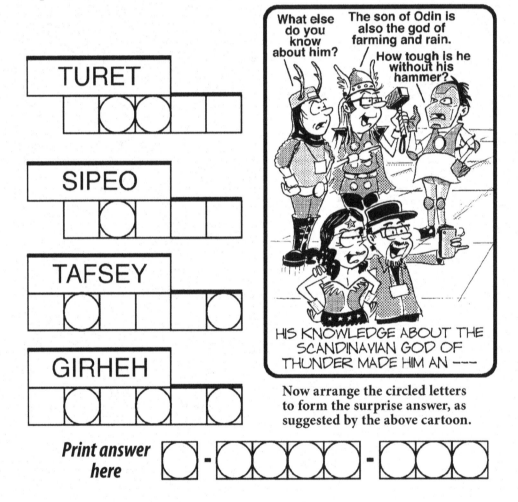

What else do you know about him?

The son of Odin is also the god of farming and rain.

How tough is he without his hammer?

HIS KNOWLEDGE ABOUT THE SCANDINAVIAN GOD OF THUNDER MADE HIM AN ---

TURET

SIPEO

TAFSEY

GIRHEH

Now arrange the circled letters to form the surprise answer, as suggested by the above cartoon.

Print answer here ⬡-⬡⬡⬡⬡-⬡⬡⬡

JUMBLE®

Unscramble these four Jumbles, one letter to each square, to form four ordinary words.

DDDEA

KARNP

DOLEMY

DUSOIT

Cool! Does it run?

Not very well. The clock works. I think it needs more potatoes.

HE INVENTED AN ENGINE FOR HIS CAR THAT RAN ON POTATOES, BUT IT JUST ----

Now arrange the circled letters to form the surprise answer, as suggested by the above cartoon.

Print answer here "◯◯◯◯◯◯◯◯◯"

JUMBLE®

Unscramble these four Jumbles, one letter
to each square, to form four ordinary words.

NERDT

BIHTA

THEWIG

ENWIRN

I need to run again. I can't seem to lose anything.

I wouldn't say that.

HE STRUGGLED
TO LOSE WEIGHT,
BUT HE DID HAVE ---

Now arrange the circled letters
to form the surprise answer, as
suggested by the above cartoon.

Print answer here

JUMBLE®

Unscramble these four Jumbles, one letter to each square, to form four ordinary words.

AKBAC

ZIPAZ

NILMEG

LETREN

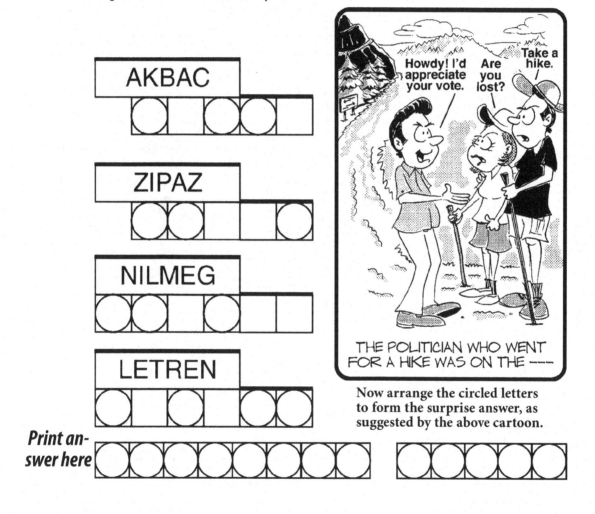

THE POLITICIAN WHO WENT FOR A HIKE WAS ON THE ----

Now arrange the circled letters to form the surprise answer, as suggested by the above cartoon.

Print answer here

JUMBLE®

Unscramble these four Jumbles, one letter to each square, to form four ordinary words.

GETAN

NIRKD

LAPWOL

COBEUN

Will you look at him!

I hear he's from Canada.

SHE WANTED TO SEE THE NEW GOOSE, SO SHE ----

Now arrange the circled letters to form the surprise answer, as suggested by the above cartoon.

Print answer here

JUMBLE®

Unscramble these four Jumbles, one letter
to each square, to form four ordinary words.

SHIKW

GEIRT

POCNAY

BARSOB

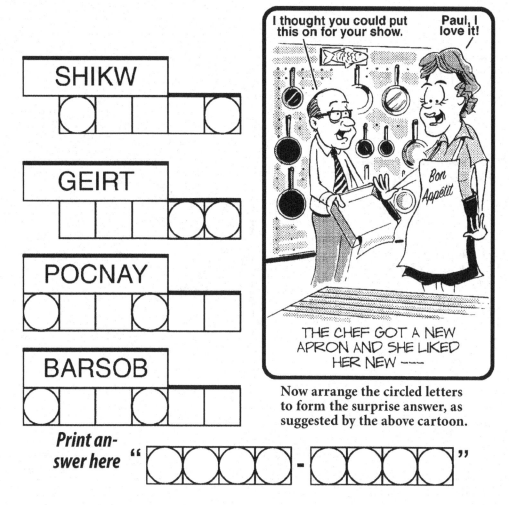

I thought you could put
this on for your show.

Paul, I
love it!

Bon
Appétit

THE CHEF GOT A NEW
APRON AND SHE LIKED
HER NEW ----

Now arrange the circled letters
to form the surprise answer, as
suggested by the above cartoon.

*Print an-
swer here* " ⬡⬡⬡⬡ - ⬡⬡⬡⬡ "

JUMBLE®

Unscramble these four Jumbles, one letter
to each square, to form four ordinary words.

NIHKT

KEJRO

LEPACA

DARISU

Here are our
famous flapjacks,
right off the
griddle.

Flappin'Jack's
Voted BEST Pancakes
in town!

I had
the
tall
stack!

THEIR PANCAKES WERE
BECOMING POPULAR
AND SELLING ----

Now arrange the circled letters
to form the surprise answer, as
suggested by the above cartoon.

*Print
answer
here*

JUMBLE®

Unscramble these four Jumbles, one letter
to each square, to form four ordinary words.

RIYAN

SOTHI

SNURKH

PREPEP

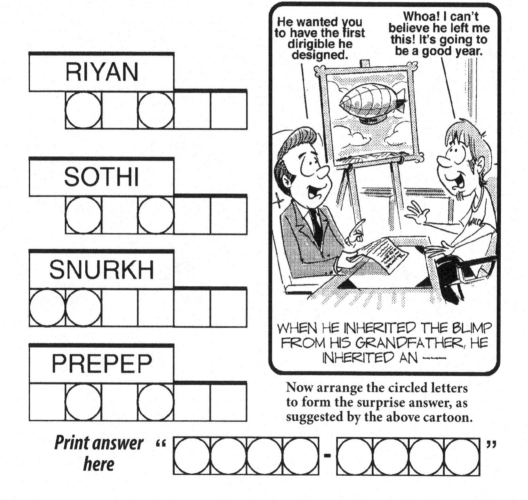

He wanted you
to have the first
dirigible he
designed.

Whoa! I can't
believe he left me
this! It's going to
be a good year.

WHEN HE INHERITED THE BLIMP
FROM HIS GRANDFATHER, HE
INHERITED AN –––

Now arrange the circled letters
to form the surprise answer, as
suggested by the above cartoon.

**Print answer
here** " ◯◯◯◯-◯◯◯◯ "

JUMBLE.

Unscramble these four Jumbles, one letter
to each square, to form four ordinary words.

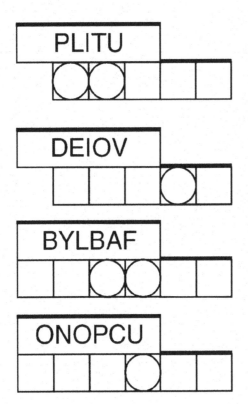

PLITU

DEIOV

BYLBAF

ONOPCU

He was great!

Like a hummingbird.

How do you think you did?

I think I nailed it!

AFTER HIS SUCCESSFUL
AUDITION, THE DRUMMER
WAS ---

Now arrange the circled letters
to form the surprise answer, as
suggested by the above cartoon.

Print answer here

JUMBLE®

Unscramble these four Jumbles, one letter to each square, to form four ordinary words.

SERDS

MENOV

GENBIN

LINKUE

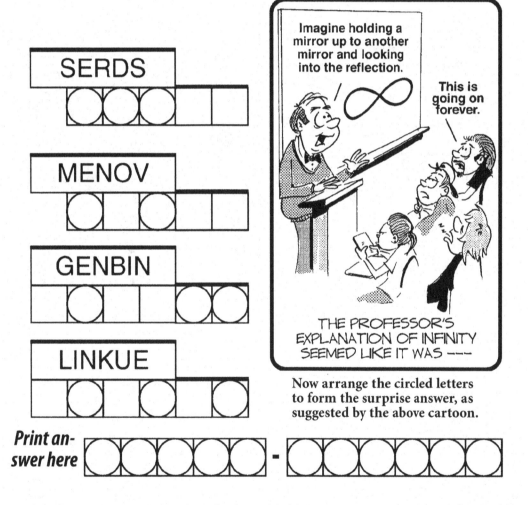

Imagine holding a mirror up to another mirror and looking into the reflection.

This is going on forever.

THE PROFESSOR'S EXPLANATION OF INFINITY SEEMED LIKE IT WAS ---

Now arrange the circled letters to form the surprise answer, as suggested by the above cartoon.

Print answer here ⬜⬜⬜⬜⬜ - ⬜⬜⬜⬜⬜⬜⬜

JUMBLE®

Unscramble these four Jumbles, one letter
to each square, to form four ordinary words.

WARND

KOGEC

WUTOTI

NNVUEE

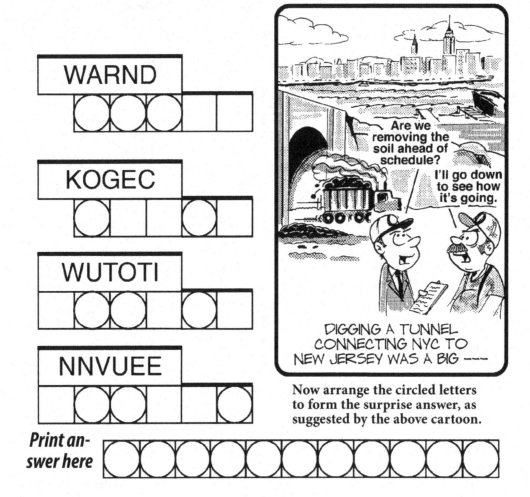

Are we removing the soil ahead of schedule?

I'll go down to see how it's going.

DIGGING A TUNNEL
CONNECTING NYC TO
NEW JERSEY WAS A BIG ----

Now arrange the circled letters
to form the surprise answer, as
suggested by the above cartoon.

*Print an-
swer here*

138

JUMBLE®

Unscramble these four Jumbles, one letter
to each square, to form four ordinary words.

OHCOP

MEAZA

PERLIP

GUFREE

Tonight,
I'll keep
working on
the corner.

Can I work
on it on
pizza
night?

Move your
plate. I think
I see one I
need.

WHEN THEY WORKED ON THE
JIGSAW PUZZLE DURING
DINNER, THEY PUT IT
TOGETHER ----

Now arrange the circled letters
to form the surprise answer, as
suggested by the above cartoon.

**Print answer
here**

JUMBLE®

Unscramble these four Jumbles, one letter
to each square, to form four ordinary words.

INONO

URTOM

SAPROT

LUUPNG

Is my milk
going to be
in a sharp
Cheddar or a
baby Swiss?

Does it matter?
Cheese is cheese.

Can
mine be
in a mild
Cheddar?

WHETHER OR NOT THE
COW'S MILK WOULD BE USED
TO MAKE CHEDDAR OR SWISS
CHEESE WAS A ----

Now arrange the circled letters
to form the surprise answer, as
suggested by the above cartoon.

*Print an-
swer here* "☐◯◯◯-◯" ☐◯◯◯◯◯

JUMBLE®

Unscramble these four Jumbles, one letter
to each square, to form four ordinary words.

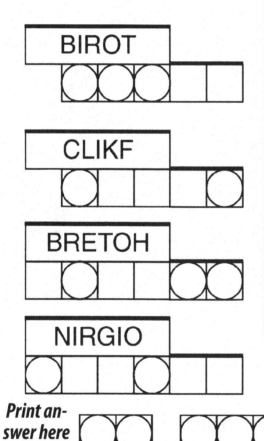

BIROT

CLIKF

BRETOH

NIRGIO

HE LOST ALL HIS MONEY
PLAYING POKER AFTER HE
DECIDED TO ----

Now arrange the circled letters
to form the surprise answer, as
suggested by the above cartoon.

**Print an-
swer here**

JUMBLE®

Unscramble these four Jumbles, one letter
to each square, to form four ordinary words.

KAHYS

NEESS

MALROC

BRUTAP

Did you find that after
winning the Irish
dance contest? Can
you get the wrinkles
out?

I'm afraid
I'll ruin it if I try.

SHE DIDN'T WANT TO IRON
HER FOUR-LEAF CLOVER
BECAUSE SHE DIDN'T WANT
TO ---

Now arrange the circled letters
to form the surprise answer, as
suggested by the above cartoon.

Print answer here

JUMBLE®

Unscramble these four Jumbles, one letter to each square, to form four ordinary words.

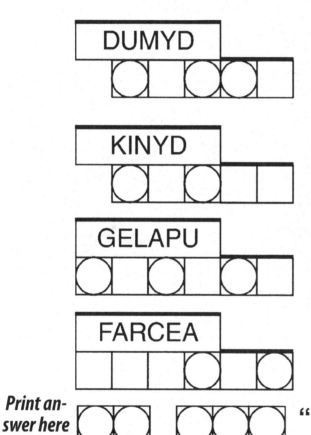

DUMYD

KINYD

GELAPU

FARCEA

Bill, I need you awake, please. Rise and shine.

1+2=
2+2=
3+2=
4+2=
5+2=

WHEN HE DOZED OFF IN THE MATH CLASS, THE TEACHER SAID ----

Now arrange the circled letters to form the surprise answer, as suggested by the above cartoon.

Print answer here

"◯◯◯ - '◯◯"

JUMBLE.

Unscramble these four Jumbles, one letter
to each square, to form four ordinary words.

TWIYT

AANER

DAYSIM

SOFUNI

This feels nice.

It takes the
chill out of the
air.

WHEN THEY HEATED SLICES
OF BREAD ON THE
CAMPFIRE, THEY WERE ----

Now arrange the circled letters
to form the surprise answer, as
suggested by the above cartoon.

*Print an-
swer here*

JUMBLE®

Unscramble these four Jumbles, one letter
to each square, to form four ordinary words.

COTBH

YEJON

MYTESS

CUEDER

What a great meal. I'm stuffed.

Honey! I thought you were on a diet?

I didn't want there to be leftovers.

IT WASN'T THE MINUTES SPENT AT THE TABLE THAT CAUSED HIS WEIGHT GAIN, IT WAS THE ---

Now arrange the circled letters
to form the surprise answer, as
suggested by the above cartoon.

Print answer here ◯◯◯◯◯◯◯◯

JUMBLE®

Unscramble these four Jumbles, one letter to each square, to form four ordinary words.

TONEF

FOREF

GEPTIL

DALIRA

The landing gear has shorted out.

We're going to be floating away soon.

THE DOWNPOUR AT THE AIRPORT TURNED THE TARMAC INTO A ---

Now arrange the circled letters to form the surprise answer, as suggested by the above cartoon.

Print answer here ⟨◯◯◯◯◯⟩ " ⟨◯◯◯◯◯⟩ "

JUMBLE

Unscramble these four Jumbles, one letter
to each square, to form four ordinary words.

CATRT

GLITH

NETYRD

DIMMUE

Oh, my gosh!
Run!

I was afraid
of this!

WHEN THE HIKERS CAME
ACROSS THE POISONOUS
SNAKE ON THE TRAIL, ---

Now arrange the circled letters
to form the surprise answer, as
suggested by the above cartoon.

*Print an-
swer here*

JUMBLE®

Unscramble these four Jumbles, one letter
to each square, to form four ordinary words.

BIHTA

PLAAH

SESVUR

DURIPT

Let's go right
between the
mainland and
the islands.

WHEN MAGELLAN NAVIGATED
AROUND THE TIP OF SOUTH
AMERICA, HIS PASSAGE WAS ----

Now arrange the circled letters
to form the surprise answer, as
suggested by the above cartoon.

Print answer here " ◯◯◯◯◯◯ " ◯◯◯◯◯

JUMBLE®

Unscramble these four Jumbles, one letter to each square, to form four ordinary words.

SASBI

INGOG

CLIFNH

NOIDWW

Wow! I hit that one right on the money.

Way to go, partner!

HER
HOLE IN ONE
RESULTED IN ----

Now arrange the circled letters to form the surprise answer, as suggested by the above cartoon.

Print answer here

JUMBLE®

Unscramble these four Jumbles, one letter
to each square, to form four ordinary words.

LIVAT

POMOH

TAWULN

KASTBE

This thing is so
uncomfortable.

It makes
you talk
funny, Ed.

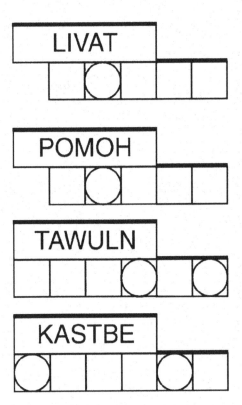

THE HORSE DIDN'T LIKE
WEARING A MOUTHPIECE. HE
DIDN'T LIKE IT ----

Now arrange the circled letters
to form the surprise answer, as
suggested by the above cartoon.

Print answer here ☐☐☐ ☐☐☐

JUMBLE®

Unscramble these four Jumbles, one letter to each square, to form four ordinary words.

LOVAC

RUFIT

XOESPE

BRYATE

Here's his new smile. Uh, maybe you should set down your coffee.

I don't like the sound of this.

WHAT SHE TOLD HER HUSBAND BEFORE HANDING HIM THE ORTHODONTIST'S BILL ---

Now arrange the circled letters to form the surprise answer, as suggested by the above cartoon.

Print answer here

JUMBLE®

Unscramble these four Jumbles, one letter to each square, to form four ordinary words.

NAPRO

KKOIS

TEENIC

TRAMWH

Do you need any help?

I've got this! It's easy.

MAKING STIR-FRIED VEGETABLES AT THE COOKOUT WAS A ---

Now arrange the circled letters to form the surprise answer, as suggested by the above cartoon.

Print an-swer here " ☐☐☐ " ☐☐ ☐☐☐ ☐☐☐☐

JUMBLE®

Unscramble these four Jumbles, one letter
to each square, to form four ordinary words.

RESUH

BUDTO

COILSA

PINNAK

We also have 40 other actors to include in our contract.

We have our own actors to add.

I don't need one!

Are you getting a speech coach?

WHEN DONALD AND DAFFY
TEAMED UP TO MAKE A
MOVIE, IT WAS A HUGE ----

Now arrange the circled letters
to form the surprise answer, as
suggested by the above cartoon.

*Print an-
swer here* " ☐☐☐ - ☐☐☐☐☐ - ☐☐☐☐ "

JUMBLE®

Unscramble these four Jumbles, one letter to each square, to form four ordinary words.

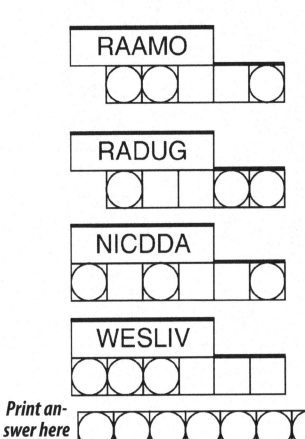

RAAMO

RADUG

NICDDA

WESLIV

I need to get back to work.

The object is to go out first.

Uno!

Uncle Jeff, you're losing!

THE JUMBLE ARTIST LOVED PLAYING UNO WITH HIS FAMILY, BUT HE DIDN'T LIKE ———

Now arrange the circled letters to form the surprise answer, as suggested by the above cartoon.

Print answer here

JUMBLE®

Unscramble these four Jumbles, one letter
to each square, to form four ordinary words.

ROLYG

MYHET

CONUBE

GELELA

It comes about every 76 years.
Halley was the first to recognize
its pattern. Have you two heard
of Mark Twain? Here's something
you may not know...

I just wanted
to know if we
could watch
"Star Wars."

HIS GRANDFATHER'S STORY
ABOUT HALLEY'S COMET
WAS A ----

Now arrange the circled letters
to form the surprise answer, as
suggested by the above cartoon.

**Print answer
here**

JUMBLE®

Unscramble these four Jumbles, one letter
to each square, to form four ordinary words.

PERAO

NETVE

FHIRTT

LOWBEB

That should block the view.

Those trees look perfect.

WHEN HE PLANTED THE
THREE OAKS SIDE BY SIDE,
HE PLANTED A ----

Now arrange the circled letters
to form the surprise answer, as
suggested by the above cartoon.

Print answer here " ⬡◯◯◯◯ - ◯ "

JUMBLE®

Unscramble these four Jumbles, one letter to each square, to form four ordinary words.

CATRT

REYDB

STAGEK

TIENIV

Hey! Someone sabotaged my equipment.

He's awful.

THE UNSCRUPULOUS MAGICIAN ATTEMPTED TO THWART HIS COMPETITION WITH ----

Now arrange the circled letters to form the surprise answer, as suggested by the above cartoon.

Print answer here

JUMBLE

Unscramble these four Jumbles, one letter
to each square, to form four ordinary words.

KAWAE

NUHOD

HONYWA

VERHIT

Yes. I see
your name
right here.
That's a good
thing.

Phew!
I'm so
relieved.

AFTER REALIZING HE
WAS AT THE PEARLY GATES,
HE SAID ----

Now arrange the circled letters
to form the surprise answer, as
suggested by the above cartoon.

Print an-
swer here

JUMBLE®

Unscramble these four Jumbles, one letter to each square, to form four ordinary words.

MLUAB

KIYLS

THIKNG

TIBNTE

Hold on. Let me write these lyrics and help Priscilla.

Honey, can you change Lisa Marie?

ELVIS GOT SO MANY THINGS DONE SIMULTANEOUSLY BECAUSE HE WAS THE ---

Now arrange the circled letters to form the surprise answer, as suggested by the above cartoon.

Print answer here " ⬡⬡⬡⬡⬡ - ⬡⬡⬡⬡ - ⬡⬡⬡⬡ "

JUMBLE®

Unscramble these four Jumbles, one letter
to each square, to form four ordinary words.

BETAA

TUCOS

REQUSA

TTNNIE

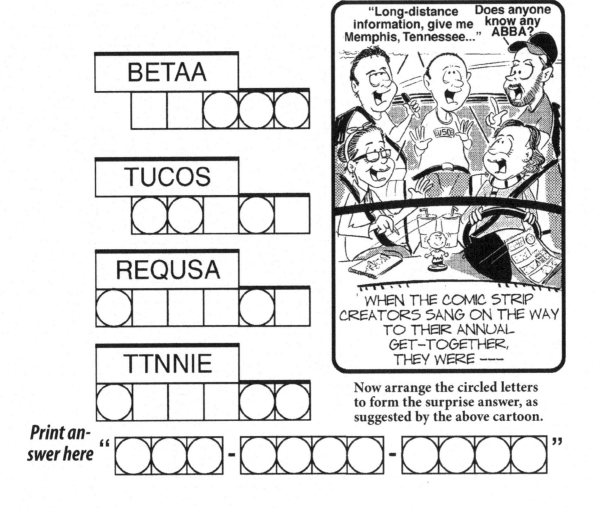

"Long-distance
information, give me
Memphis, Tennessee..."

Does anyone
know any
ABBA?

WHEN THE COMIC STRIP
CREATORS SANG ON THE WAY
TO THEIR ANNUAL
GET-TOGETHER,
THEY WERE ----

Now arrange the circled letters
to form the surprise answer, as
suggested by the above cartoon.

*Print an-
swer here* " ◯◯◯ - ◯◯◯◯ - ◯◯◯◯ "

JUMBLE®

Unscramble these four Jumbles, one letter
to each square, to form four ordinary words.

GANTY

LIHYL

DOYBON

MIRLEB

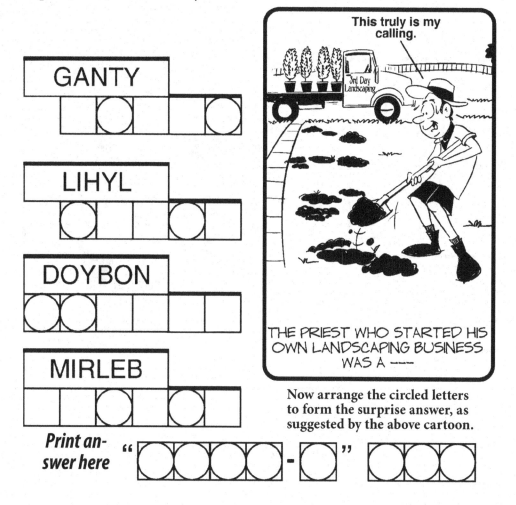

This truly is my calling.

3rd Day Landscaping

THE PRIEST WHO STARTED HIS
OWN LANDSCAPING BUSINESS
WAS A ----

Now arrange the circled letters
to form the surprise answer, as
suggested by the above cartoon.

Print answer here " ◯◯◯◯◯ - ◯ " ◯◯◯◯

JUMBLE®

Unscramble these four Jumbles, one letter
to each square, to form four ordinary words.

WYENL

NAXEN

ETIRVD

TALWEL

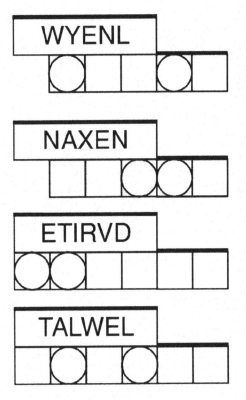

100 Acres

For Sale

Pond!

150 Acres

Thank you for
calling ParSell
Properties.
How may I help
you?

THE REAL ESTATE AGENT WHO
SPECIALIZED IN SELLING LARGE
TRACTS OF PROPERTY,
HAD A ---

Now arrange the circled letters
to form the surprise answer, as
suggested by the above cartoon.

Print answer here

JUMBLE®
UNLEASHED

Challenger Puzzles

JUMBLE®

Unscramble these six Jumbles, one letter
to each square, to form six ordinary words.

REHOYT

SCONEH

RANDOG

SENLOS

RNMEAN

ANNTFI

Seriously?
I had our
child four
months ago!

Are you
being
funny?

What do I know?
I'm going bald.
See? I lost five
more strands.

AFTER MAKING A JOKE
ABOUT HIS WIFE'S WEIGHT
GAIN, HE'D NEED TO
TRY TO ---

Now arrange the circled letters
to form the surprise answer, as
suggested by the above cartoon.

Print answer here

JUMBLE®

Unscramble these six Jumbles, one letter to each square, to form six ordinary words.

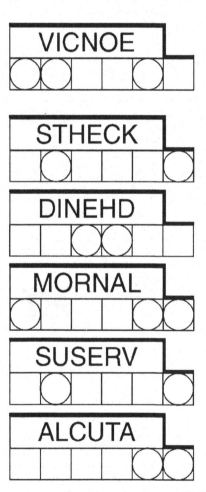

VICNOE

STHECK

DINEHD

MORNAL

SUSERV

ALCUTA

It's good to see everyone topside, having fun.

Trip aces!

I have a straight!

WHEN PLAYING POKER ON THE NAVY SHIP, IT WAS ---

Now arrange the circled letters to form the surprise answer, as suggested by the above cartoon.

Print answer here

JUMBLE®

Unscramble these six Jumbles, one letter
to each square, to form six ordinary words.

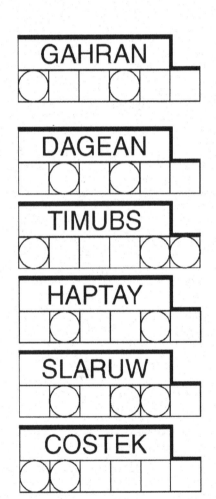

GAHRAN

DAGEAN

TIMUBS

HAPTAY

SLARUW

COSTEK

Wow. That was fast.

I didn't even catch his name.

Time for you to move on.

What! I've only been here for one game!

Kid. This is never easy to do.

THE NEW QB WAS
BEING TRADED AFTER
ONLY ONE GAME.
HE WAS JUST ----

Now arrange the circled letters
to form the surprise answer, as
suggested by the above cartoon.

Print answer here

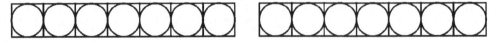

JUMBLE

Unscramble these six Jumbles, one letter to each square, to form six ordinary words.

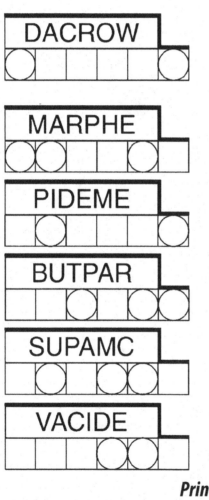

DACROW

MARPHE

PIDEME

BUTPAR

SUPAMC

VACIDE

My old friend Andy sold this to me for $1, after I told him I loved tomato soup. Now, I'm giving it to you.

I can't even imagine how much it's worth now.

Like it! We love it! Thank you!

We love tomato soup, too! Thanks!

Tomato SOUP

WHEN HER GRANDFATHER GAVE THEM SUCH A VALUABLE PAINTING, IT WAS ---

Now arrange the circled letters to form the surprise answer, as suggested by the above cartoon.

Print answer here

JUMBLE®

Unscramble these six Jumbles, one letter
to each square, to form six ordinary words.

PRUINT

DOHLSU

TERPEM

WAMODE

KICEWT

LATEHH

Great! I didn't
buy milk and
eggs because of
your forecast.

Hey! You said
the blizzard
would miss us!

Sorry, fellas.
I'll get it
right, next
time.

THE METEOROLOGIST WAS
TAKING SOME HEAT FOR
NOT PREDICTING THE
BLIZZARD, BUT HE'D ———

Now arrange the circled letters
to form the surprise answer, as
suggested by the above cartoon.

Print answer here

JUMBLE®

Unscramble these six Jumbles, one letter to each square, to form six ordinary words.

LOFWOL

OLDEOD

ROTMLA

SPEMIO

PUCAHB

PETTIO

I can see the mountain ranges! It's unbelievable.

It goes on forever.

WHEN HE LOOKED THROUGH HIS NEW TELESCOPE, HE THOUGHT THE VIEW WAS ----

Now arrange the circled letters to form the surprise answer, as suggested by the above cartoon.

Print answer here

JUMBLE®

Unscramble these six Jumbles, one letter
to each square, to form six ordinary words.

ANRUDO

OMBYED

TOBYNA

TACILI

LICDAP

LUUFES

Have they started framing yet?

I told my dad about this show. He loves it.

I've watched it since it started.

THE HOME IMPROVEMENT
SHOW BECAME SO POPULAR
BECAUSE IT WAS ABLE TO ----

Now arrange the circled letters
to form the surprise answer, as
suggested by the above cartoon.

Print answer here

JUMBLE®

Unscramble these six Jumbles, one letter to each square, to form six ordinary words.

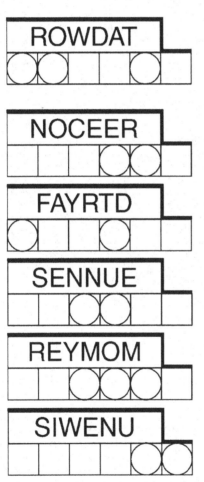

ROWDAT

NOCEER

FAYRTD

SENNUE

REYMOM

SIWENU

Who wants cake?

I love that we have a bigger table now.

Now we can have parties.

I do! I'm still hungry.

I'll have ice cream too!

THEIR HOME'S NEW ADDITION INCLUDED A LARGER EATING AREA. THEY NOW HAD ---

Now arrange the circled letters to form the surprise answer, as suggested by the above cartoon.

Print answer here

JUMBLE®

Unscramble these six Jumbles, one letter to each square, to form six ordinary words.

TENNIY

CLEOLA

RUBADS

TISNIS

CRADOC

BLUMYH

THE RUDE POOL PLAYER WASN'T LIKED VERY MUCH. EVERYONE THOUGHT HE HAD ---

Now arrange the circled letters to form the surprise answer, as suggested by the above cartoon.

Print answer here

JUMBLE®

Unscramble these six Jumbles, one letter to each square, to form six ordinary words.

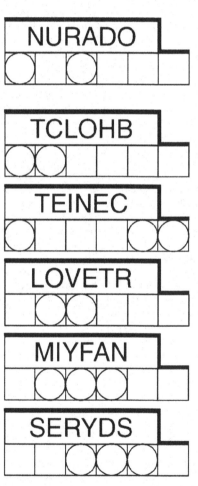

NURADO

TCLOHB

TEINEC

LOVETR

MIYFAN

SERYDS

Well, I think our job here is done.

Yep. We deserve a break from photosynthesis.

FOLIAGE HAS A STEADY JOB ON TREES UNTIL THE ----

Now arrange the circled letters to form the surprise answer, as suggested by the above cartoon.

Print answer here

" ⬡⬡⬡⬡⬡⬡⬡ " ⬡⬡ ⬡⬡⬡⬡⬡⬡⬡

JUMBLE®

Unscramble these six Jumbles, one letter to each square, to form six ordinary words.

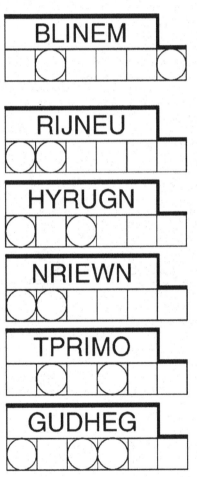

BLINEM

RIJNEU

HYRUGN

NRIEWN

TPRIMO

GUDHEG

Why don't we go for a walk and get your mind off this?

I keep thinking there's something more I can do.

HIS LACK OF SUCCESS DIETING AND EXERCISING WAS ———

Now arrange the circled letters to form the surprise answer, as suggested by the above cartoon.

Print answer here

JUMBLE®

Unscramble these six Jumbles, one letter to each square, to form six ordinary words.

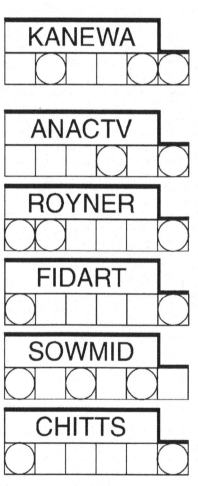

KANEWA

ANACTV

ROYNER

FIDART

SOWMID

CHITTS

I love being so close to the pond.

Let me have a rock. I'll skip it from up here.

IT'S EASY TO SKIP ROCKS ON A POND WHEN THE POND IS A ---

Now arrange the circled letters to form the surprise answer, as suggested by the above cartoon.

Print answer here

JUMBLE®

Unscramble these six Jumbles, one letter
to each square, to form six ordinary words.

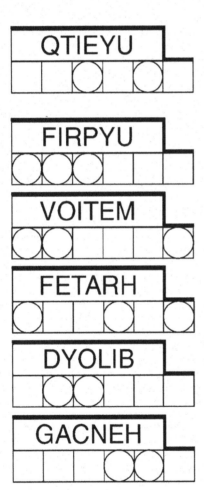

QTIEYU

FIRPYU

VOITEM

FETARH

DYOLIB

GACNEH

We're off to
a great
start.

FAMILY
TREE
NURSERY

I'm so glad our
family gave us
seed money to
get this going.

THEY BUILT
THEIR PLANT
NURSERY ---

Now arrange the circled letters
to form the surprise answer, as
suggested by the above cartoon.

Print answer here

176

JUMBLE®

Unscramble these six Jumbles, one letter
to each square, to form six ordinary words.

TLHIGF

YENONA

LUWANT

CLNIFH

CERADA

GROFEA

THE TENNIS PLAYER
THREW HIS RACKET
AFTER HE ---

Now arrange the circled letters
to form the surprise answer, as
suggested by the above cartoon.

Print answer here

JUMBLE®

Unscramble these six Jumbles, one letter
to each square, to form six ordinary words.

ROALCM

HERWNC

TUPEYD

WIHELA

NEDALT

AHDORI

Claire, you seemed fine on the way up to Kilimanjaro's summit.

It started after we reached the peak.

THE MOUNTAIN CLIMBER STARTED SNEEZING AND COUGHING AT THE SUMMIT, AND ———

Now arrange the circled letters
to form the surprise answer, as
suggested by the above cartoon.

Print answer here

JUMBLE

Unscramble these six Jumbles, one letter to each square, to form six ordinary words.

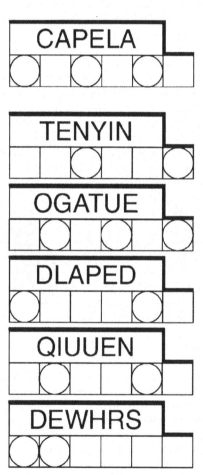

CAPELA

TENYIN

OGATUE

DLAPED

QIUUEN

DEWHRS

You've got two chances: slim and none. And slim just left town. You couldn't jab your way out of a paper bag.

You talk tough. We'll see when you hit the floor with your head.

THE BOXER WAS VERY OUTSPOKEN ABOUT HIS OPPONENT AND DIDN'T ---

Now arrange the circled letters to form the surprise answer, as suggested by the above cartoon.

Print answer here

JUMBLE®

Unscramble these six Jumbles, one letter to each square, to form six ordinary words.

BONGLO

TREELT

LIBEVA

CASESC

IQIDUL

GCYANE

Though your tests indicated this would be unthinkable, you're going to have quadruplets.

How is this possible?

I don't believe it!

THEY WERE SHOCKED WHEN THEY FOUND OUT THEY WERE HAVING QUADRUPLETS. IT SEEMED ----

Now arrange the circled letters to form the surprise answer, as suggested by the above cartoon.

Print answer here

JUMBLE®

Unscramble these six Jumbles, one letter
to each square, to form six ordinary words.

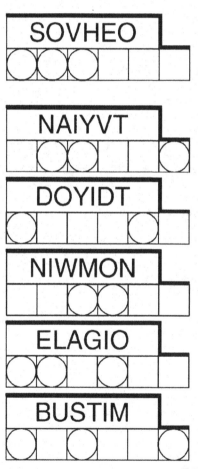

SOVHEO

NAIYVT

DOYIDT

NIWMON

ELAGIO

BUSTIM

Who do you
think you are—
Sergio Garcia?

I'm going
for it!

DID HIS WIFE THINK
HE'D BE ABLE TO REACH
THE GREEN MORE THAN
300 YARDS AWAY? ---

Now arrange the circled letters
to form the surprise answer, as
suggested by the above cartoon.

Print answer here

JUMBLE®

Unscramble these six Jumbles, one letter
to each square, to form six ordinary words.

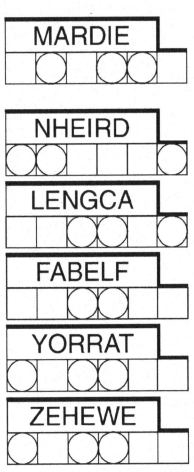

MARDIE

NHEIRD

LENGCA

FABELF

YORRAT

ZEHEWE

Do you want people
to think they're
watching a cartoon?

You weren't
complaining
when our ratings
were up.

SUNNY
TODAY

72°

THE METEOROLOGIST
TURNED ON HIS
CO-WORKER BECAUSE
HE WAS A ----

Now arrange the circled letters
to form the surprise answer, as
suggested by the above cartoon.

Print answer here

JUMBLE

Unscramble these six Jumbles, one letter to each square, to form six ordinary words.

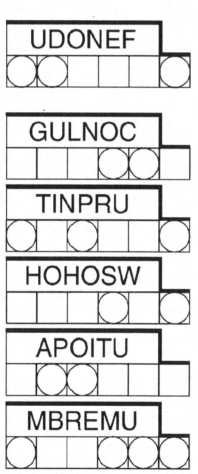

UDONEF

GULNOC

TINPRU

HOHOSW

APOITU

MBREMU

What have you dug up? Is it the soil?

I'd like to test down here for pollution.

TO FIND OUT WHY HIS APPLE TREES WERE DYING, HE NEEDED TO GET TO THE ---

Now arrange the circled letters to form the surprise answer, as suggested by the above cartoon.

Print answer here

Answers

1. **Jumbles:** WAGON SHEEP WHOLLY SURETY
    Answer: Such recruits have no business getting fresh—"RAW" ONES

2. **Jumbles:** UNWED FOLIO BARREL SURELY
    Answer: It was awful—until a letter arrived to make it "legal"!—"L-AWFUL"

3. **Jumbles:** AWASH TULLE PENCIL BEAUTY
    Answer: Where his wife sent him—"UP THE WALL"

4. **Jumbles:** PAYEE LINGO HEALTH TEMPER
    Answer: What stories heard during a flight are expected to be—ON A HIGH PLANE

5. **Jumbles:** AROMA HENCE COUSIN JOBBER
    Answer: She wanted the pin, but hesitated to do this—"BROOCH" IT

6. **Jumbles:** HUSKY WAGER MOTION MILDEW
    Answer: A pretty low form of life might get ahead when he does this—WORM HIS WAY

7. **Jumbles:** BAKED ADAPT WEDGED GARISH
    Answer: What "changed" when the snow melted?—"THAW"

8. **Jumbles:** AORTA BIPED BANDIT MATRON
    Answer: It may be the cause of a kid's running away from home—AN ERRAND

9. **Jumbles:** MEALY CUBIT NEARBY MODEST
    Answer: Out of jail—and ill in bed—"B-AIL-ED"

10. **Jumbles:** LINER MINUS CHARGE PENMAN
    Answer: Metal devices that help keep locks in place—HAIRPINS

11. **Jumbles:** AMUSE TITLE JINGLE BIGAMY
    Answer: What a girl sometimes wears at the beach—A BAITING SUIT

12. **Jumbles:** KNEEL LAUGH IMBIBE JOCKEY
    Answer: They called him a colorful fighter because he was this most of the time—BLACK & BLUE

13. **Jumbles:** TULIP CHALK OXYGEN QUIVER
    Answer: How to dress on a very cold day—QUICKLY

14. **Jumbles:** CASTE MONEY ANYHOW BOILED
    Answer: Why the cops couldn't catch up with the pickpocket—HE STOLE AWAY

15. **Jumbles:** WOMEN JUICE ALWAYS BICKER
    Answer: What those hoboes were telling—"BUM" JOKES

16. **Jumbles:** QUEER BARGE INJURY FORCED
    Answer: What the heavy smoker was advised to do—REDUCE

17. **Jumbles:** HOUSE EATEN GARISH ACHING
    Answer: What one mouse said to the other as he saw the trap being baited—"CHEESE IT"

18. **Jumbles:** NAIVE AROMA PANTRY GARLIC
    Answer: An article of clothing a gentleman might have around the arm—"G-ARM-ENT"

19. **Jumbles:** AFTER PIKER JOYFUL MALLET
    Answer: What the gambler named his daughter—KITTY

20. **Jumbles:** MOLDY ORBIT HARDLY MEASLY
    Answer: Ran off with a roll of cloth—"BOLT-ED"

21. **Jumbles:** OPIUM COLON BELONG GOITER
    Answer: What's the royal road to marriage?—GOING TO "COURT"

22. **Jumbles:** DRAFT CHAMP PHYSIC ENTICE
    Answer: What that "swell" guy had—A HEAD TO MATCH

23. **Jumbles:** HENCE SKIMP DEFAME SEETHE
    Answer: What a mermaid is—A DEEP SHE-FISH

24. **Jumbles:** NEWLY GNARL TIMELY SUBMIT
    Answer: You might serve it to others, but you wouldn't want to eat it yourself—A TENNIS BALL

25. **Jumbles:** LOVER DITTO VERSUS MOHAIR
    Answer: What a souped-up car that broke down was—A "SHOT" ROD

26. **Jumbles:** RIGOR BOUGH WEAKEN BLOODY
    Answer: Why the bookworm visited the library—TO "BURROW" A BOOK

27. **Jumbles:** FOIST LOFTY DEFILE PICKET
    Answer: What two words have the most letters in them?—POST OFFICE

28. **Jumbles:** ELUDE JOUST MEMBER INJURE
    Answer: What you might see when a big elephant squirts water from his trunk—A JUMBO JET

29. **Jumbles:** LEAKY COMET SCHEME OPPOSE
    Answer: What slot machines produce for their owners—XX

30. **Jumbles:** EAGLE MOTIF BEWARE GENDER
    Answer: What the cattle raiser did when he got a bum steer—BEEFED ABOUT IT

31. **Jumbles:** GUISE FETID BIGAMY FACTOR
    Answer: What he said when he heard his neighbor had bought one of those new computers—IT FIGURES!

32. **Jumbles:** PLUME KAPOK IMPEDE SCHOOL
    Answer: What the timid soul finally did when his bicycle wheel collapsed—"SPOKE" UP

33. **Jumbles:** NUTTY FLORA WISDOM DEBATE
    Answer: What that filibusterer in the Senate was throwing—HIS "WAIT" AROUND

34. **Jumbles:** AZURE CLOTH BARIUM ELICIT
    Answer: What the man from Prague called his wife—HIS "CZECH" MATE

35. **Jumbles:** DOUBT BERET ABUSED HOMING
    Answer: Would you expect a man who has a finger in a big transportation deal to do this?—THUMB A RIDE

36. **Jumbles:** GAUGE DIRTY NETHER INDOOR
    Answer: Who was that ghost who appeared at the door?—A DEAD RINGER

37. **Jumbles:** HEDGE SIXTY ZIGZAG NEWEST
    Answer: For a sweater, he thought this was the right size—THE TIGHT SIZE

38. **Jumbles:** GUEST AROMA DELUGE GUNNER
    Answer: What some backseat drivers never seem to do—RUN OUT OF GAS

39. **Jumbles:** KNACK DITTY COOPER FETISH
    Answer: How to brighten up your boyfriend's evening—SIT IN THE DARK

40. **Jumbles:** LEGAL BOOTH ADRIFT MARROW
    Answer: What the blind date she was looking forward to meeting turned out to be—A "DREAM BLOAT"

41. **Jumbles:** GRIPE POISE JACKAL PEWTER
    Answer: What the judge gave the guy who was arrested for stealing a watch—THE "WORKS"

42. **Jumbles:** RHYME AUDIT HAMPER FRENZY
    Answer: If she ever told her real age, her birthday cake would be this—A FIRE HAZARD

43. **Jumbles:** APRON WRATH ELDEST BURLAP
    Answer: In order to find out which kind of ice-cream soda is the best, take this—A "STRAW" POLL

44. **Jumbles:** FLOUR AGING INTACT LEDGER
    Answer: Her face is her fortune, and it runs into this—A NICE FIGURE

45. **Jumbles:** DOUGH GLOVE MOBILE INCOME
    Answer: Needed to impress a laundress—A GOOD LINE

46. **Jumbles:** BRAVE HONEY ANYHOW CUDGEL
Answer: He had a "peach" of a secretary until his wife ordered this—HER "CANNED"

47. **Jumbles:** PRIME DIZZY SUPERB JUMPER
Answer: What he often did behind his wife's back—ZIPPED HER UP

48. **Jumbles:** BIRCH CLOUT FELONY HIDING
Answer: Why his ex-wife took him to the cleaners—HE WAS FILTHY RICH

49. **Jumbles:** RIGOR NUDGE OPENLY ARTFUL
Answer: They resented that ritzy pooch because he always wanted to do this —PUT ON THE DOG

50. **Jumbles:** CYNIC HAVEN CORPSE BUMPER
Answer: Ways that go straight to the heart—VEINS

51. **Jumbles:** IDIOT CHEEK POETRY DRIVEL
Answer: How he protested when they put him in the cooler—HOTLY

52. **Jumbles:** BROOD MOLDY COMPEL NOVICE
Answer: The snob was insulted when the doctor told him he was merely suffering from this—A "COMMON" COLD

53. **Jumbles:** MADLY PIKER OPPOSE BICEPS
Answer: It might be "ill-gotten"—SICK PAY

54. **Jumbles:** MOUNT EJECT LATEST THROAT
Answer: Might be three that could put you out—"ETHER"

55. **Jumbles:** RIVET VIPER INVITE LAUNCH
Answer: The warden guaranteed the entertainers that the audience would be this—A "CAPTIVE" ONE

56. **Jumbles:** EXCEL PANIC NEPHEW ANKLET
Answer: Could it be a place to live if you've got time?—A CELL

57. **Jumbles:** SNACK PIPER MASCOT NICELY
Answer: They hush up reports of murders—SILENCERS

58. **Jumbles:** YACHT OPERA INWARD ASSAIL
Answer: This musical composition "involves" harps at first—"RHAPS-ODY"

59. **Jumbles:** CARGO FOCUS UPSHOT TROPHY
Answer: What the rookie G.I. was told to take in order to get to the barber's in the quickest possible way—A SHORT CUT

60. **Jumbles:** BARON LOFTY SUBMIT GRISLY
Answer: What "Jack and the Beanstalk" is—A TALL STORY

61. **Jumbles:** BORAX FORTY PELVIS OPAQUE
Answer: Could be a sport "connected" with the clergy—"PASTOR"

62. **Jumbles:** TASTY ARDOR YEARLY BOUGHT
Answer: What they paid the king who wrote a book—A ROYALTY

63. **Jumbles:** TRIPE HOVEL STOOGE OUTFIT
Answer: What the guy who stole a banana gave the cops—THE SLIP

64. **Jumbles:** MAKER NAVAL PALATE UPWARD
Answer: Could it have been a drama about a famous fleet?—"ARMADA"

65. **Jumbles:** GROIN BERTH HOOKED STOLEN
Answer: What he was, after he bought her that big diamond—STONE-BROKE

66. **Jumbles:** HELLO BASIC AFFRAY CAUGHT
Answer: What kind of a guy was that press photographer?—A FLASHY ONE

67. **Jumbles:** LOVER FLAME POLITE MISLAY
Answer: He works out the problems of "mixed-up" lovers—"SOLVER"

68. **Jumbles:** TONIC STOOP POISON COUSIN
Answer: Everything you should know about entrances and exits—THE INS & OUTS

69. **Jumbles:** GOING DEMON PHYSIC FACADE
Answer: What that mutt liked best for breakfast—"POOCHED" EGGS

70. **Jumbles:** FAVOR DEITY MOTION APIECE
Answer: What the Greek god did when one of the goddesses brought him his drink—"NECTAR"

71. **Jumbles:** COUGH IRATE AUTUMN FIDDLE
Answer: What time is it when clothes wear out?—RAGTIME

72. **Jumbles:** OUNCE DAILY FOURTH PASTRY
Answer: What they called that intellectual hobo—THE "ROAD SCHOLAR"

73. **Jumbles:** KNIFE SWISH GUITAR FORCED
Answer: What ice on the road is—SKID STUFF

74. **Jumbles:** FACET CHAFE MUSTER EXHALE
Answer: Many a "true" word is spoken between them—FALSE TEETH

75. **Jumbles:** CHALK THYME LAYOFF DETAIN
Answer: Skiing is a wintertime sport often learned thus—IN THE "FALL"

76. **Jumbles:** AWARD EXTOL COOKIE SEXTON
Answer: What happened when that body builder put a tight T-shirt on his torso?—IT TORE SO

77. **Jumbles:** CROWN BERET EASILY ZENITH
Answer: What the mad chef was—STIR CRAZY

78. **Jumbles:** ABBEY FABLE ABLAZE BEAUTY
Answer: What a fat cat is—A FLABBY TABBY

79. **Jumbles:** UNIFY BATHE FLORAL CORNEA
Answer: What there was when the king of beasts led a breakout from the zoo—A "REBEL-LION"

80. **Jumbles:** PIOUS HARPY CANINE DROWSY
Answer: What turtle soup is—A SNAPPY DISH

81. **Jumbles:** INEPT BAKED ANEMIA TRUSTY
Answer: Sales resistance is the triumph of this—MIND OVER PATTER

82. **Jumbles:** FEIGN MOCHA DAHLIA GENIUS
Answer: What that pretty girl whose boyfriend kept her waiting was—A CHAFING "DISH"

83. **Jumbles:** REBEL DIRTY FAMISH LACKEY
Answer: How she loved the cardiologist—WITH ALL HER HEART

84. **Jumbles:** CREEK MAXIM ASYLUM FLAXEN
Answer: What the robber said as he made his getaway —"SAFE" BY A MILE

85. **Jumbles:** NOISY GNOME SUBWAY KETTLE
Answer: Even more fun than having a vacation is having this—THE BOSS TAKE ONE

86. **Jumbles:** CATCH HEFTY FIZZLE GARBLE
Answer: What the guy who thought he was a wit was—ONLY HALF RIGHT

87. **Jumbles:** CHESS UNWED MISERY WALNUT
Answer: She admitted she was forty but she didn't do this—SAY WHEN

88. **Jumbles:** SOGGY ABASH PUZZLE RAVAGE
Answer: What he said that so-called barley soup was—BARELY SOUP

89. **Jumbles:** SHOWY WOMEN JACKET ALWAYS
Answer: What the talking cat said every time its master returned home—WHAT'S "MEW"?

90. **Jumbles:** JOKER MONEY PRAYER VALUED
Answer: What the down-and-out poet did—"ODE" EVERYONE

91. **Jumbles:** SWAMP BANJO RENDER MAGPIE
Answer: At what age were they married?—AT THE "PARSON-AGE"

92. **Jumbles:** GIVEN TWILL BAMBOO INFIRM
Answer: What the solitary pawnbroker undoubtedly was—A "LOANER"

93. **Jumbles:** BUILT MANGY JOVIAL TRYING
Answer: Could this be why he was a jailbird?—"ROBIN"

94. **Jumbles:** CHIME GAUGE BOUNCE FALLOW
Answer: Some people who think they're very funny are really just this—LAUGHABLE

95. **Jumbles:** DECAY BALMY DELUGE PREFIX
Answer: Women a confirmed bachelor learns to avoid—"BRIDE-EYED" ONES

96. **Jumbles:** SINGE DOUGH CEMENT SINFUL
Answer: The trombone player was fired because he did this—LET THINGS SLIDE

97. **Jumbles:** NUTTY SAUTE JACKAL ORATOR
Answer: What they told at the foot doctors' annual shindig—"CORNY" JOKES

98. **Jumbles:** JOLLY LYING LAYMAN FLIMSY
Answer: Another name for horse meat—FILLY MIGNON

99. **Jumbles:** POKED DANDY NOBODY BIGAMY
Answer: What business was at the dynamite factory—BOOMING

100. **Jumbles:** BRAWL DUMPY HERALD RAGLAN
Answer: What it might be when you gambol across the street—A GAMBLE

101. **Jumbles:** CEASE PAVED TAVERN TRENDY
Answer: Everyone doing the tango at the club was in—"ATTEND-DANCE"

102. **Jumbles:** FLACK RATIO SHOULD POTENT
Answer: He wanted to learn how to play golf, so he—TOOK A COURSE

103. **Jumbles:** VOWEL TWICE TACKLE RADIUM
Answer: When Noah designed his huge boat, he was an—"ARK-ITECT"

104. **Jumbles:** NINTH FORGO REMOVE NOTION
Answer: They hadn't yet decided which new house to buy, but they were—HOMING IN ON ONE

105. **Jumbles:** AGAIN CARGO MEADOW MODULE
Answer: When they ran out of lettuce for salads, he told the kitchen staff to—"ROMAINE" CALM

106. **Jumbles:** MUSTY VENOM ROBBER ORIGIN
Answer: In the 1950's, 45 RPM records became so popular because people thought they were—GROOVY

107. **Jumbles:** GRIME HOUND NATIVE VIABLE
Answer: When it came to learning how to swim, she was ready to—DIVE RIGHT IN

108. **Jumbles:** INEPT PUTTY ONWARD VERSUS
Answer: They wanted more information about the mountain they'd just climbed, so they—READ UP ON IT

109. **Jumbles:** HEDGE MOUTH MEMORY WEASEL
Answer: The owner of the Hawaiian sugar plantation was—HOME SWEET HOME

110. **Jumbles:** AWFUL UNWED ORIOLE UNPAID
Answer: The Wikipedia page about the history of the limbo featured the—LOW-DOWN

111. **Jumbles:** VALET BEACH SIDING LUNACY
Answer: Everyone watching the 4th of July fireworks display was—HAVING A BLAST

112. **Jumbles:** FUDGE PROVE LEGEND JUSTLY
Answer: Flying on the cramped plane to Italy left them—JET "LEGGED"

113. **Jumbles:** PERCH PRONE CONVEY TARTAR
Answer: The high price of their pasta dinner in Florence cost them a—PRETTY PENNE

114. **Jumbles:** POISE FEIGN COHORT IMPACT
Answer: They asked the reporter where to buy the best gelato, so they could—GET THE SCOOP

115. **Jumbles:** SEIZE HANDY PUTRID ZOMBIE
Answer: When the customer at the Italian eatery got angry, he gave the owner a—"PIZZA" OF HIS MIND

116. **Jumbles:** HOUSE GUAVA NOTIFY MARROW
Answer: Seeing Roman ruins all day was this for the teenagers—ENOUGH "FORUM"

117. **Jumbles:** KOALA PILOT GROUCH HOLLER
Answer: Going through the gift shop at the museum was a—PACKAGE TOUR

118. **Jumbles:** HUMUS ICING ABSORB DEFECT
Answer: To pay for the new roof support system, he used his—"TRUSS" FUND

119. **Jumbles:** ADULT CRUSH FREELY HEREBY
Answer: After seeing how angry the male cow was, she decided to—STEER CLEAR

120. **Jumbles:** SALAD BRING PLUNGE FERVOR
Answer: Hundreds of millions of cars have crossed the Golden Gate Bridge, thanks to its—LONG LIFE SPAN

121. **Jumbles:** YOUNG VOUCH UNEVEN HARDLY
Answer: The affectionate pigeons were—LOVEY-DOVEY

122. **Jumbles:** WHINE ALIAS AFRAID FLIMSY
Answer: Locking up their valuables in the wall behind the painting didn't work because it wasn't—FAIL-SAFE

123. **Jumbles:** WOUND STUNT ADJOIN PARODY
Answer: The owners of the new plant nursery had no plans to ever move and wanted to—PUT DOWN ROOTS

124. **Jumbles:** CAMEO ACUTE KOSHER HERMIT
Answer: When he paired the two players, the tennis pro was a—MATCHMAKER

125. **Jumbles:** WAVER RURAL APPEAR MOTIVE
Answer: His moving business really started to take off when the number of jobs started to—RAMP UP

126. **Jumbles:** UTTER POISE SAFETY HIGHER
Answer: His knowledge about the Scandinavian god of thunder made him an—A-THOR-ITY

127. **Jumbles:** ADDED PRANK MELODY STUDIO
Answer: He invented an engine for his car that ran on potatoes, but it just—"SPUDDERED"

128. **Jumbles:** TREND HABIT WEIGHT WINNER
Answer: He struggled to lose weight, but he did have—THINNING HAIR

129. **Jumbles:** ABACK PIZZA MINGLE RELENT
Answer: The politician who went for a hike was on the—CAMPAIGN TRAIL

130. **Jumbles:** AGENT DRINK WALLOP BOUNCE
Answer: She wanted to see the new goose, so she—TOOK A GANDER

131. **Jumbles:** WHISK TIGER CANOPY ABSORB
Answer: The chef got a new apron and she liked her new—"COOK-WEAR"

132. **Jumbles:** THINK JOKER PALACE RADIUS
Answer: Their pancakes were becoming popular and selling—LIKE HOTCAKES

133. **Jumbles:** RAINY HOIST SHRUNK PEPPER
Answer: When he inherited the blimp from his grandfather, he inherited an—"HEIR-SHIP"

134. **Jumbles:** TULIP VIDEO FLABBY COUPON
Answer: After his successful audition, the drummer was—UPBEAT

135. **Jumbles:** DRESS VENOM BENIGN UNLIKE
Answer: The professor's explanation of infinity seemed like it was—NEVER-ENDING

136. **Jumbles:** DRAWN GECKO OUTWIT UNEVEN
Answer: Digging a tunnel connecting NYC to New Jersey was a big—UNDERTAKING

137. **Jumbles:** POOCH AMAZE RIPPLE REFUGE
Answer: When they worked on the jigsaw puzzle during dinner, they put it together—PIECEMEAL

138. **Jumbles:** ONION TUMOR PASTOR UNPLUG
Answer: Whether or not the cow's milk would be used to make cheddar or Swiss cheese was a—"MOO-T" POINT

186

139. **Jumbles:** ORBIT FLICK BOTHER ORIGIN
Answer: He lost all his money playing poker after he decided to—GO FOR BROKE

140. **Jumbles:** SHAKY SENSE CLAMOR ABRUPT
Answer: She didn't want to iron her four-leaf clover because she didn't want to—PRESS HER LUCK

141. **Jumbles:** MUDDY DINKY PLAGUE CARAFE
Answer: When he dozed off in math class, the teacher said—UP AND "ADD-'EM"

142. **Jumbles:** WITTY ARENA DISMAY FUSION
Answer: When they heated slices of bread on the campfire, they were—WARM AND TOASTY

143. **Jumbles:** BOTCH ENJOY SYSTEM REDUCE
Answer: It wasn't the minutes spent at the table that caused his weight gain, it was the—SECONDS

144. **Jumbles:** OFTEN OFFER PIGLET RADIAL
Answer: The downpour at the airport turned the tarmac into a—FLOOD "PLANE"

145. **Jumbles:** TRACT LIGHT TRENDY MEDIUM
Answer: When the hikers came across the poisonous snake on the trail,—IT RATTLED THEM

146. **Jumbles:** HABIT ALPHA VERSUS PUTRID
Answer: When Magellan navigated around the tip of South America, his passage was—"STRAIT" AHEAD

147. **Jumbles:** BASIS GOING FLINCH WINDOW
Answer: Her hole in one resulted in—SWING DANCING

148. **Jumbles:** VITAL OOMPH WALNUT BASKET
Answer: The horse didn't like wearing a mouthpiece. He didn't like it—ONE BIT

149. **Jumbles:** VOCAL FRUIT EXPOSE BETRAY
Answer: What she told her husband before handing him the orthodontist's bill—BRACE YOURSELF

150. **Jumbles:** APRON KIOSK ENTICE WARMTH
Answer: Making stir-fried vegetables at the cookout was a—"WOK" IN THE PARK

151. **Jumbles:** USHER DOUBT SOCIAL NAPKIN
Answer: When Donald and Daffy teamed up to make a movie, it was a huge—"PRO-DUCKS-TION"

152. **Jumbles:** AROMA GUARD CANDID SWIVEL
Answer: The Jumble artist loved playing UNO with his family, but he didn't like—DRAWING CARDS

153. **Jumbles:** GLORY THYME BOUNCE ALLEGE
Answer: His grandfather's story about Halley's Comet was a—LONG TALE

154. **Jumbles:** OPERA EVENT THRIFT WOBBLE
Answer: When he planted the three oaks side by side, he planted a—"TREE-O"

155. **Jumbles:** TRACT DERBY GASKET INVITE
Answer: The unscrupulous magician attempted to thwart his competition with—DIRTY TRICKS

156. **Jumbles:** AWAKE HOUND ANYHOW THRIVE
Answer: After realizing he was at the Pearly Gates, he said—OH, THANK HEAVEN

157. **Jumbles:** ALBUM SILKY KNIGHT BITTEN
Answer: Elvis got so many things done simultaneously because he was the—"MULTI-TASK-KING"

158. **Jumbles:** ABATE SCOUT SQUARE INTENT
Answer: When the comic strip creators sang on the way to their annual get-together, they were—"CAR-TUNE-ISTS"

159. **Jumbles:** TANGY HILLY NOBODY LIMBER
Answer: The priest who started his own landscaping business was a—"HOLE-Y" MAN

160. **Jumbles:** NEWLY ANNEX DIVERT WALLET
Answer: The real estate agent who specialized in selling large tracts of property, had a—LANDLINE

161. **Jumbles:** THEORY CHOSEN DRAGON LESSON MANNER INFANT
Answer: After making a joke about his wife's weight gain, he'd need to try to—LIGHTEN THE MOOD

162. **Jumbles:** NOVICE SKETCH HIDDEN NORMAL VERSUS ACTUAL
Answer: When playing poker on the Navy ship, it was—ALL HANDS ON DECK

163. **Jumbles:** HANGAR AGENDA SUBMIT APATHY WALRUS SOCKET
Answer: The new QB was being traded after only one game. He was just—PASSING THROUGH

164. **Jumbles:** COWARD HAMPER IMPEDE ABRUPT CAMPUS ADVICE
Answer: When her grandfather gave them such a valuable painting, it was—MUCH APPRECIATED

165. **Jumbles:** TURNIP SHOULD TEMPER MEADOW WICKET HEALTH
Answer: The meteorologist was taking some heat for not predicting the blizzard, but he'd—WEATHER THE STORM

166. **Jumbles:** FOLLOW DOODLE MORTAL IMPOSE HUBCAP TIPTOE
Answer: When he looked through his new telescope, he thought the view was—OUT OF THIS WORLD

167. **Jumbles:** AROUND EMBODY BOTANY ITALIC PLACID USEFUL
Answer: The home improvement show became so popular because it was able to—BUILD AN AUDIENCE

168. **Jumbles:** TOWARD ENCORE DRAFTY UNSEEN MEMORY UNWISE
Answer: Their home's new addition included a larger eating area. They now had—ROOM FOR DESSERT

169. **Jumbles:** NINETY LOCALE ABSURD INSIST ACCORD HUMBLY
Answer: The rude pool player wasn't liked very much. Everyone thought he had—BAD TABLE MANNERS

170. **Jumbles:** AROUND BLOTCH ENTICE REVOLT INFAMY DRESSY
Answer: Foliage has a steady job on trees until the—"LEAVES" OF ABSENCE

171. **Jumbles:** NIMBLE INJURE HUNGRY WINNER IMPORT HUGGED
Answer: His lack of success dieting and exercising was—WEIGHING ON HIM

172. **Jumbles:** AWAKEN VACANT ORNERY ADRIFT WISDOM STITCH
Answer: It's easy to skip rocks on a pond when the pond is a—STONE'S THROW AWAY

173. **Jumbles:** EQUITY PURIFY MOTIVE FATHER BODILY CHANGE
Answer: They built their plant nursery—FROM THE GROUND UP

174. **Jumbles:** FLIGHT ANYONE WALNUT FLINCH ARCADE FORAGE
Answer: The tennis player threw his racket after he—FLEW OFF THE HANDLE

175. **Jumbles:** CLAMOR WRENCH DEPUTY AWHILE DENTAL HAIRDO
Answer: The mountain climber started sneezing and coughing at the summit, and—CAME DOWN WITH A COLD

176. **Jumbles:** PALACE NINETY OUTAGE PADDLE UNIQUE SHREWD
Answer: The boxer was very outspoken about his opponent and didn't—PULL ANY PUNCHES

177. **Jumbles:** OBLONG LETTER VIABLE ACCESS LIQUID AGENCY
Answer: They were shocked when they found out they were having quadruplets. It seemed—INCONCEIVABLE

178. **Jumbles:** HOOVES VANITY ODDITY MINNOW GOALIE SUBMIT
Answer: Did his wife think he'd be able to reach the green more than 300 yards away?—NO…NOT BY A LONG SHOT

179. **Jumbles:** ADMIRE HINDER GLANCE BAFFLE ROTARY WHEEZE
Answer: The meteorologist turned on his co-worker because he was a—FAIR-WEATHER FRIEND

180. **Jumbles:** FONDUE UNCLOG TURNIP WHOOSH UTOPIA BUMMER
Answer: To find out why his apple trees were dying, he needed to get to the—ROOT OF THE PROBLEM

Need More Jumbles®?

Order any of these books through your bookseller or call Triumph Books toll-free at 800-335-5323.

Jumble® Books

More than 175 puzzles each!

Cowboy Jumble®
ISBN: 978-1-62937-355-3

Jammin' Jumble®
ISBN: 1-57243-844-4

Java Jumble®
ISBN: 978-1-60078-415-6

Jazzy Jumble®
ISBN: 978-1-57243-962-7

Jet Set Jumble®
ISBN: 978-1-60078-353-1

Joyful Jumble®
ISBN: 978-1-60078-079-0

Juke Joint Jumble®
ISBN: 978-1-60078-295-4

Jumble® Anniversary
ISBN: 987-1-62937-734-6

Jumble® at Work
ISBN: 1-57243-147-4

Jumble® Ballet
ISBN: 978-1-62937-616-5

Jumble® Birthday
ISBN: 978-1-62937-652-3

Jumble® Celebration
ISBN: 978-1-60078-134-6

Jumble® Circus
ISBN: 978-1-60078-739-3

Jumble® Cuisine
ISBN: 978-1-62937-735-3

Jumble® Drag Race
ISBN: 978-1-62937-483-3

Jumble® Ever After
ISBN: 978-1-62937-785-8

Jumble® Explorer
ISBN: 978-1-60078-854-3

Jumble® Explosion
ISBN: 978-1-60078-078-3

Jumble® Fever
ISBN: 1-57243-593-3

Jumble® Fiesta
ISBN: 1-57243-626-3

Jumble® Fun
ISBN: 1-57243-379-5

Jumble® Galaxy
ISBN: 978-1-60078-583-2

Jumble® Garden
ISBN: 978-1-62937-653-0

Jumble® Genius
ISBN: 1-57243-896-7

Jumble® Geography
ISBN: 978-1-62937-615-8

Jumble® Getaway
ISBN: 978-1-60078-547-4

Jumble® Gold
ISBN: 978-1-62937-354-6

Jumble® Grab Bag
ISBN: 1-57243-273-X

Jumble® Gymnastics
ISBN: 978-1-62937-306-5

Jumble® Jackpot
ISBN: 1-57243-897-5

Jumble® Jailbreak
ISBN: 978-1-62937-002-6

Jumble® Jambalaya
ISBN: 978-1-60078-294-7

Jumble® Jamboree
ISBN: 1-57243-696-4

Jumble® Jitterbug
ISBN: 978-1-60078-584-9

Jumble® Journey
ISBN: 978-1-62937-549-6

Jumble® Jubilation
ISBN: 978-1-62937-784-1

Jumble® Jubilee
ISBN: 1-57243-231-4

Jumble® Juggernaut
ISBN: 978-1-60078-026-4

Jumble® Junction
ISBN: 1-57243-380-9

Jumble® Jungle
ISBN: 978-1-57243-961-0

Jumble® Kingdom
ISBN: 978-1-62937-079-8

Jumble® Knockout
ISBN: 978-1-62937-078-1

Jumble® Madness
ISBN: 1-892049-24-4

Jumble® Magic
ISBN: 978-1-60078-795-9

Jumble® Marathon
ISBN: 978-1-60078-944-1

Jumble® Neighbor
ISBN: 978-1-62937-845-9

Jumble® Parachute
ISBN: 978-1-62937-548-9

Jumble® Safari
ISBN: 978-1-60078-675-4

Jumble® See & Search
ISBN: 1-57243-549-6

Jumble® See & Search 2
ISBN: 1-57243-734-0

Jumble® Sensation
ISBN: 978-1-60078-548-1

Jumble® Surprise
ISBN: 1-57243-320-5

Jumble® Symphony
ISBN: 978-1-62937-131-3

Jumble® Theater
ISBN: 978-1-62937-484-03

Jumble® University
ISBN: 978-1-62937-001-9

Jumble® Unleashed
ISBN: 978-1-62937-844-2

Jumble® Vacation
ISBN: 978-1-60078-796-6

Jumble® Wedding
ISBN: 978-1-62937-307-2

Jumble® Workout
ISBN: 978-1-60078-943-4

Jumpin' Jumble®
ISBN: 978-1-60078-027-1

Lunar Jumble®
ISBN: 978-1-60078-853-6

Monster Jumble®
ISBN: 978-1-62937-213-6

Mystic Jumble®
ISBN: 978-1-62937-130-6

Outer Space Jumble®
ISBN: 978-1-60078-416-3

Rainy Day Jumble®
ISBN: 978-1-60078-352-4

Ready, Set, Jumble®
ISBN: 978-1-60078-133-0

Rock 'n' Roll Jumble®
ISBN: 978-1-60078-674-7

Royal Jumble®
ISBN: 978-1-60078-738-6

Sports Jumble®
ISBN: 1-57243-113-X

Summer Fun Jumble®
ISBN: 1-57243-114-8

Touchdown Jumble®
ISBN: 978-1-62937-212-9

Travel Jumble®
ISBN: 1-57243-198-9

TV Jumble®
ISBN: 1-57243-461-9

Oversize Jumble® Books

More than 500 puzzles each!

Generous Jumble®
ISBN: 1-57243-385-X

Giant Jumble®
ISBN: 1-57243-349-3

Gigantic Jumble®
ISBN: 1-57243-426-0

Jumbo Jumble®
ISBN: 1-57243-314-0

The Very Best of Jumble® BrainBusters
ISBN: 1-57243-845-2

Jumble® Crosswords™

More than 175 puzzles each!

More Jumble® Crosswords™
ISBN: 1-57243-386-8

Jumble® Crosswords™ Jackpot
ISBN: 1-57243-615-8

Jumble® Crosswords™ Jamboree
ISBN: 1-57243-787-1

Jumble® BrainBusters™

More than 175 puzzles each!

Jumble® BrainBusters™
ISBN: 1-892049-28-7

Jumble® BrainBusters™ II
ISBN: 1-57243-424-4

Jumble® BrainBusters™ III
ISBN: 1-57243-463-5

Jumble® BrainBusters™ IV
ISBN: 1-57243-489-9

Jumble® BrainBusters™ 5
ISBN: 1-57243-548-8

Jumble® BrainBusters™ Bonanza
ISBN: 1-57243-616-6

Boggle™ BrainBusters™
ISBN: 1-57243-592-5

Boggle™ BrainBusters™ 2
ISBN: 1-57243-788-X

Jumble® BrainBusters™ Junior
ISBN: 1-892049-29-5

Jumble® BrainBusters™ Junior II
ISBN: 1-57243-425-2

Fun in the Sun with Jumble® BrainBusters™
ISBN: 1-57243-733-2